THE WORLD'S #1
BEST SELLING SOCCER BOOK

BY
KEN AND STEVE LAITIN

with the assistance of Lindy Laitin

cover design: Ron Norris

SOCCER FOR AMERICANS
Box 836
Manhattan Beach, California 90266

DEDICATION

To our grandparents, Jerome and Shirley Laitin and Eugene and Miriam Watson. With thanks for their love and encouragement.

Photo Credits:
Dave Graefe
John Kagdis
Oto Maxmilian

Library of Congress Number 79-63980
ISBN 0-916802-13-2

Soccer for Americans
Box 836
Manhattan Beach, California 90266

Here we are, about three years before we kicked our first soccer ball.

TABLE OF CONTENTS

Part Three
RESTARTS: WHEN THE BALL IS NOT IN PLAY

Part Four
PROBLEMS

Part Five
STORIES

Part Six
THINKING SERIOUSLY ABOUT SOCCER

Part Seven
WORDS YOU SHOULD KNOW 114

With our Mother and Dad, discussing, talking soccer.

INTRODUCTION

If you are new to soccer, we wrote this book to help you!

When we first got started in soccer we felt very lost, since there is so much to learn. After a while we learned enough to have fun and not to feel lost. This we hope to pass on to you. There is always more to learn in soccer. We learn at soccer camps, soccer clinics, team practices and in games. No matter how long you play you will always be learning and, we hope, having fun.

Paul Harris suggested that we could help new players by telling them why and how to do things. Before we wrote this book, we talked a lot to each other. For each skill we asked each other questions and wrote down the answers. Then we tested what we had written by teaching the skills and tactics to our nine-year-old sister, Lindy.

If you want to be a good soccer player we have four tips for you:

(1) At all times know what you want to do in the game. Keep asking yourself: "If the ball comes to me, what will I do with it? If the ball goes to that player on the other team, what will I do?"

(2) Be aggressive. Say: "That is my ball, and I'm going to get it and keep it away from the other team." Try to be first on the ball and two out of three times you will be first.

(3) Practice your skills, especially passing and shooting. Start easy and build up.

(4) Get in shape and keep in shape. If you and your team are in shape, you'll be able to keep playing for longer and you will score, especially in the last quarter of the game.

DO YOU REALLY WANT TO PLAY SOCCER?

For us, soccer has been great. We have lots of fun. We have built up our strength, speed and endurance. Practicing for soccer has helped us to improve for other sports, too. Building our leg muscles has helped us in baseball and swimming. Jumping and leaping have helped us in basketball. We have found that when we became good at a sport, it became more fun to play.

Here is Steve during his first baseball season. Soccer has helped us build our leg muscles for baseball.

We have made many new friends, and have had many experiences which we will remember for years to come. When we played on the Roadrunners, we made the State Championship Playoffs. We traveled to San Francisco and played a game at the Stanford University Stadium. It was fun to fly up as a group and to visit a large university. After the game, we drove around the city and had a pizza party. Also, we played in the Los Angeles Coliseum. Other teams we've been on have played in preliminary games that took place before the professional games of the North American Soccer League's Los Angeles Aztecs and of the American Soccer League's Los Angeles Skyhawks. We have also played a

preliminary game in the Los Angeles Coliseum against a youth team from a town near Mexico City. It sure was a lot of fun to play in front of a large number of fans and to share experiences with the boys from the other teams.

You, too, can have fun playing soccer. Most kids like to kick a ball around, but kicking it around with skill takes a lot of work. You will have to run a lot in your game, and will have to do a lot of running at your team practices. This you may find boring. Since you will have to be able to move quickly and turn quickly, you will have to practice different kinds of movements, and do them again and again, until you get good and quick at them. Since you will have to control and pass the ball, you will have to spend many hours learning and practicing skills. While many of these skills can be practiced in little group games which are fun, other skills do not lend themselves to fun-type games.

To become a good soccer player takes time and effort. Soccer is a good sport, because it's the kind of sport where anyone can play. Size does not matter. All that matters is whether you really want to improve your skills.

We hope that you will like soccer well enough to want to play it. We wrote this book to help you. We would like to share with you what we have learned about positions and team play. We would like to share with you what we have learned about skills. But, most of all, we would like to share some of the fun experiences we have had through soccer. We hope that when you play, you will find soccer a fun game too, and that you will also make friends and have the same kind of adventures that we have had.

4

WHEN YOU START TO PLAY:
FIRST, GET THE BIG PICTURE

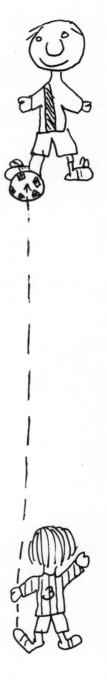

Congratulations, you are a member of a soccer team! Being on a team means you will be working together with other players. Every player on your team is important! Every player on your team will have specific jobs to do. And, everyone on your team must also be prepared to help everyone else on your team to do his job.

When you play soccer, if you know what you want to do on the field and if you try hard to do it, then you will be well on your way to becoming a good player. The more you play and the more you practice, the more you will develop your skills. But, this takes time, so have patience.

Here's Ken during an important game. He was probably thinking: "That's my ball, and I'm going to get it."

Remember that a large part of how well you play depends on your attitude and on your state of mind. If you keep thinking, "That's my ball — I'm going to get it — and I'm going to pass it where I want it to go," then more than half the time you will beat your opponent to the ball. If you think positively and if you play aggressively, you'll enjoy soccer and soon your individual and team skills will improve.

Every member of your team will play an assigned position. Different coaches and different books call the various positions by different names. Basically, there are (1) the goalie, (2) the defenders, (3) the midfielders and (4) the forwards.

The Goalie

The goalie patrols the penalty area. He is your team's last line of defense. He is the only player who can use his hands within the field of play. When he is in the penalty area, he has some special privileges. When he is outside the penalty area, he is just like any other player.

The goalie's job is to keep the ball from going into the goal if it is shot towards the goal. Whether the ball is in the air or loose on the ground, his job is to either get possession of it or to hit it to where it won't be a danger to his team. He does this by jumping for the ball and hitting or catching it or by throwing himself on top of it.

The goalie goes out to attacking players when the attacking player has broken past all of the defenders. The goalkeeper can see the whole field. He has the best view of the incoming attack. Thus, the goalkeeper has another important job. He gives instructions to the fullbacks about closing gaps and covering attackers.

When the goalkeeper touches or gets possession of the ball, he has to put it back into play. Thus, the goalie has to learn how to kick and throw the ball so that it clears out of the goal area in a way that keeps it out of the possession of the attacking players.

The Defenders

Most people call the defenders "fullbacks." Most of the time there will be three or four of them. You may hear the terms right fullback, left fullback, center fullback and sweeper. If you do, ask your coach to explain to you exactly what he expects that position to do. If you are a defender, then your job is to stop the other team from shooting at your goal. If they can't shoot at your goal, then they can't score. When the other team has the ball, make sure you keep yourself between the ball and your goal. If an opposing player enters your area, cover him. This means that you stay close enough to him and between him and the ball so that if the ball is passed to him you stop him from receiving the pass.

So this is what the coach meant when He said I was to play sweeper

Go to the ball. If the ball is loose, charge after it without waiting. If a player on the other team has the ball and is dribbling toward your area, go toward him and stay between him and the goal. Try to make him kick or dribble to the outside of the field. Practice taking the ball away from a player who dribbles. Learn how to tackle and how to shoulder charge. If you get the ball, kick it to the outside, away from your goal. If the play is toward the fullback next to you, be prepared to back him up in case he is beaten. Don't let the player on the other team beat you. Remember: (1) keep yourself between the ball and your goal; (2) charge after the ball without waiting; (3) force the player with the ball to the outside; (4) when defending your goal, kick the ball to the outside; (5) don't let the player with the ball shoot toward your goal; (6) back up the other defenders.

Midfielders

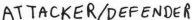

ATTACKER/DEFENDER

I'm a midfielder. I have two jobs: I attack and defend.

Another position you might play is halfback or midfielder. When you play midfielder, you are both a defender and an attacker. Your job is to stop the other team from moving the ball through your area. You also try to start the offense for your team. When the other team has the ball, your job is either to cover the open man or to get into position between the ball and your goal. You have to get into position fast when the other team is advancing. You also have to be prepared to back up the other midfielders and the fullbacks.

When you get the ball, start the offense for your team. You should either make short passes to another midfielder or to one of your forwards or you should make a long pass to an open forward. As a midfielder, you will be watching your forwards as they move in and out and around the goal area, and you will try to put the ball to a part of the field where they can get it.

Sometimes it looks awkward when you must do anything to keep the other team from getting the ball.

8

SHORT PASSES CAN BE VERY USEFUL!

Remember: When you play halfback you are defending. Always keep yourself between the ball and your own goal, or you should be covering an offensive player. Always back up the other halfbacks and your fullbacks. Always go towards the ball without waiting for it. When you have the ball, pass it. And, also practice your throw-ins. Try to make them long and accurate so that they reach the forwards or the other halfbacks.

Forwards

You may be assigned as a forward. Different teams use different numbers of forwards when they play. Usually a team will have at least three forwards and no more than five. The forwards who play towards the outside of the field are often called wingers. Wingers take the ball and dribble it towards the outside of the field and then they either try to push the ball down the wing past the defenders or they try to cross it

towards the center of the field in front of the net. If your team is good at heading, then the winger's job is to put the ball in the goal area, near the goal mouth, but far enough away from the goal to be out of the reach of the goalie.

If the ball is on the other side of the field, then the winger tries to move to open space to receive a long pass. If you play in the middle of the forward line, you are called a striker. The striker's job is to score goals. Since the play in front of the net is very fast, you have to be prepared to strike immediately and not fiddle around with the ball. If you are a striker, you should get really good at "heading".

Also, you should learn how to chest the ball and how to kick the ball right away so a defender can't get between you and the goal. When your team is on the defense, most of the forwards should go towards the middle of the field or even into your own defensive area. You should be close enough to your own halfbacks and fullbacks to receive a pass, but not too close. Your coach may want one or two forwards to hang close to the other team's goal.

When the other team has the ball, you still have a job to do. That is to help your halfbacks get the ball from them. When your team has the ball, your job is to move the ball forward and to keep possession of it. Don't be a ball hog. Pass the ball before you lose it. Bring the ball forward, and pass to an open player and then drive in at the goal. If the ball is loose, go after it. Don't wait for it because, while you are waiting for it, someone from the other team will be running for it. When you get near the goal, anytime you are open and inside the penalty area, shoot quickly for the goal. Don't shoot at the goalie. If the other team gets the ball, fall back quickly when the goalie is going to kick it out or when there is a goal kick. Lots of times you can get possession of the ball, drive it back in and score. Be aggressive.

Be careful not to get off-side. We'll cover this later.

As your team plays together more and more, your team will learn how to work together. It is important for all the players to talk to each other. This helps each player on your team to know what the other players are going to do. Call for the ball when you're open. It is especially important for the goalie to call for the ball when he wants it in a loud enough voice so that his fullbacks know he can handle the situation.

OFFSIDE

It is also important for you always to remember that soccer is a TEAM SPORT. When you are on offense, passing the ball to the open player and moving it down the field gives your team a good chance to score goals. If somebody hogs the ball or if somebody doesn't pass the ball to an open player, then your team will be hurt. But the player that isn't a "team player" is also hurting himself, since he will have fewer chances to handle the ball during a game and thus will have fewer chances to improve his skill. If your team is on the defense, then be prepared to back up your teammates.

After you understand what you are trying to accomplish as a player, then the skills you practice will have more meaning and more use. Remember that all the skills in the world will not substitute for determination.

MY FIRST COACH
by Ken

I started playing soccer when I was 7 years old. My parents registered me late in a group called the American Youth Soccer Organization, or AYSO for short. My parents took me to the home of the West Torrance Third Division Commissioner for my tryout. I had never even seen a soccer ball before. He asked me to dribble, and I didn't know what he was talking about. He showed me how to do these things, but I still didn't know what he was talking about. However, since in AYSO "Everyone plays," I was accepted and assigned to a team.

That night we got a telephone call from the coach. He told us that practice would be at 9:30 the next morning at Victor School. I was so happy I couldn't sleep. I got up real early so I wouldn't be late. Even though the school was only on the next block, our whole family drove over. When we got there we didn't see anybody. We wondered if we were at the right place. We looked all around. Finally we saw a group of boys sitting down next to a building on the other side of the field. My Father told me to run over and see if that was my team. I started to run as fast as I could. I took about 15 steps and tripped and fell right on my face. My Dad looked at my Mom and said, "Well, it's only $15. If it doesn't work out, we can always drop him out." My Mom answered, "What a way to begin!"

When I ran over to the group the man in charge said, "You must be Kenny Laitin." I answered, "Yes, I am." The man said, "I'm your coach, and this is your team, the Roadrunners." He then said to the team, "This is Kenny Laitin. Kenny will be playing with us for the rest of the year." I looked around. All the boys looked so big.

The coach had us get up and form into groups of four. He showed us how to pass the ball and had us pass the ball around. I didn't do so well, so the coach stayed next to me. All the boys said nice things like, "You sure do learn fast" and "Nice kick." The coach told me I was a natural left-footer, and that is very rare. I liked him and I liked the team.

Later that day my Father asked me how the practice had gone. I told him I liked it even though I didn't know whether I did or didn't like it. I asked my Father if he would buy me a ball so I could practice. The coach had said that everyone should have their own ball so that they could practice at home.

I went to every team practice. I made sure I got there early. I really wanted to be part of the Roadrunner Team. After several practices, the coach called all the boys around. He had me stand up. He gave me the Roadrunner pin and shook my hand. All the boys clapped. I felt very happy. Now I was really a Roadrunner. I ran all the way home to show the pin to my family.

13

Getting Started With the Roadrunners

I tried hard, but I wasn't very good. I was too young to realize how bad I really was. Every time I tried hard, even if I missed the ball, and every time I kicked the ball the older kids on the team and the coach would say something nice like, "Good Kenny," or "good kick, Kenny."

I was a substitute and played only ten minutes in each game. The first position I played was right - fullback. I really wanted to have the ball come in my direction. When the ball finally came my way, I felt very excited. Usually I was able to do what I was supposed to and would kick the ball away and towards the outside. Later on I played center - halfback. This was a good position for me because both the left - halfback and right - halfback were very strong players. They would cover for me if I was slow or if I made a mistake.

Here I am reporting to the referee after my very first goal with the Roadrunners. I wanted to make sure he had my name on his card!

Near the end of the season, the coach put me at center-forward. In one practice game near the end of the season he told me and all the boys on the team that he wanted me to score a goal. All during the game everybody passed the ball to me. Every time anybody on my team got the ball, everyone else would yell to him: "Pass to Kenny!" Everybody wanted me to score. I shot at the goal several times. My first shot came close. It bounced off the right goal post. My second shot was caught by the goalie. My third shot was a hard one to the right corner. It was on its way into the goal when the other team's left - fullback made a really good play and deflected the ball. This gave us a corner kick. While we scored on the corner kick, I wasn't the guy who put the ball in the net.

I didn't score in that game, but I scored in the very next game. Until I scored my first goal everyone on the team did everything they could to help me. When I finally scored, they were all very happy for me. The coach turned to my parents and said, "See, I told you he'd do it."

I was so happy I ran into the goal, picked up the ball and ran over to the referee to make sure he had my name right.

About the middle of the season my parents bought my younger brother, Steve, a pair of soccer shoes. We had to shop all over Torrance, Palos Verdes and the entire South Bay to find a pair small enough for him. From then on, every practice Steve would come with me to the field. He'd carry his shoes and put them on at the field, and he'd be really careful not to wear down the cleats. He would run laps and do all the exercises with the Roadrunners. He watched everything we did. Soon he also began to do the skills drills with us.

When we played practice games, he would wait and wait, hoping to be asked to play in the game. One day we broke the team into two halves for a full-field practice game. The coach asked some of the kids who were playing nearby and Steve if they wanted to play in the practice. Steve was happy to play. Steve was so happy to be asked that he told my parents about the game again and again for the next several days.

THE VIKINGS ARE COMING
by Steve

When I was 7 years old, I was finally old enough to join a soccer team. I had been waiting for this since I was 5.

I would be in a league with kids from the age of 7 to the age of 9. Since my older brother, Kenny, was 9, I would play for whatever team he was drafted on to. This team turned out to be named "The Vikings".

The Vikings, on paper, looked like about the third best team in the league, but our first practice made us look like the worst. Most of the team had never played before, or had only played for one year. Two of our players had their arms in slings and our goalie had hurt his foot and had to play in one soccer boot and one sneaker. Fortunately, we had a good coach, and some good assistant coaches (one of them was my Dad) who knew a lot about soccer.

Here's the Vikings! That's Mother and Dad, back row in the left. Lindy is fourth from right, bottom row. Ken is far right, bottom row, Steve next to Lindy.

We practiced three times a week, and we practiced hard! We went over all the special things like corner kicks, goal kicks, throw-ins, and kick-offs. My

16

brother, Kenny, and Steve Baaden took all the free kicks. We practiced these things so much that we scored on a lot of our corner kicks, and cleared, but kept possession of most of our goal kicks.

The Vikings were undefeated through the first half of the season, mainly because we had a strong attacking center half, Steve Baaden, and the league's leading scorer, my brother, Kenny, at center forward. We were also undefeated through the second half of the season, but now we were playing well together as a team and were feeling better as a team, too.

We won our League Championship and now we had to play for the Regional Championship. The game was a 0 - 0 tie, so we went into overtime and then into sudden death. We could have easily lost the game by making the slightest mistake. But the game was still tied, so we went into penalty kicks. Since it was getting dark, it was agreed that each team would take their five kicks together. By the luck of the coin toss, we went first. Since we had been practicing penalty kicks all year, we had a little edge. We made all five of our penalty kicks, and then they missed their first one. So we had won our Region and would move on to the State Championship.

We won the rest of the games pretty easily except for one game. In this game we went into the second half losing 2 - 1, and we didn't score again until Steve Baaden caught their goalie out of position and scored with a shot from about mid-field. After that, our spirits were high. Our third goal came moments later, and we had only two more games left.

The next game was pretty easy. The win put us into the Championship game. The Vikings had come the whole season without losing or tieing any games. We weren't about to lose our last game.

17

We were to play our State Championship game at El Camino College against a team from San Fransico. They were a pretty good team, but not good enough to beat the power of the Vikings. We scored both our goals on corner kicks and won the California State Championship by a score of 2 - 0.

The first goal of the State Championship game, on a corner kick. That's Ken on the left, already running toward midfield. He scored.

The whole year, from the very first practice, we had practiced corner kicks, and now it had paid off. We had two corner kicks, and we scored from them both, in the most important game of our season. We won that year because we practiced, and we practiced like a team. We went from third best in our league to first best in the State. There were no arguments; the Vikings were a team!!

18

YOU CAN'T PLEASE EVERYONE

Every coach has his own way of playing the game. So does every assistant coach. And so do many parents.

When you play, you'll get lots of advice from the sidelines. For example, when you are under pressure and just barely able to kick the ball away from an advancing forward, someone is sure to yell, "Trap it! Trap the ball! Control it first!" Other times you'll be told to play the ball by some and to hold your position by others. This yelling bugs some kids and messes up the play of others. You should try to only listen to your coach and assistant coach and to follow their instructions.

Steve going after a ball near the corner flag. The spectators and the coach are all thinking different things about what he should do.

Sometimes, if you have a new coach the things he tells you to do may not always be right. You should still listen to him unless something critical happens, like a guy on the other team about to score a goal. In this case, you should use your own judgment.

19

Sometimes a kid will talk back to his coach. Like when the coach told one of our players to move on the ball, he stopped playing, turned around and pointed at our right halfback and said, "He's a lamer. Tell him to pass it good." This kind of talking back can break up the team.

Sometimes things your coach may try won't work out, and you may think you know a better way. One of our coaches kept having us throw the ball into the middle of the field. He wanted us to get the ball and kick it to the other side of the field. Every time we tried to do it, the other team got the ball. In this case we asked our coach whether he thought we should have more of our guys come in closer to the thrower on the throw-in, or whether we should throw down the wing for a while. He answered, "Why don't you take turns trying both?"

If you make suggestions this way, most coaches will listen, and in this way you won't seem like a wise guy.

When you play soccer, there is one important person who you have to please — that is yourself. If you think you have played hard, if you have improved, then you should be pleased.

We are pleased because we have fun.

THE GAME

In soccer the main object is to score in the other team's goal, and to stop the other team from scoring in your goal. At the end of the game the team with the most goals wins.

To accomplish this purpose, players on a soccer team take up different positions on the field. As we mentioned before, each different position has a job that goes with it. During a game players on one team pass the ball to each other and try to keep the other team from getting it. When the team gets close to the goal they are attacking, they will shoot the ball at the goal to try to score. To score, the ball has to go between the goal posts and under the crossbar. The entire ball must be over the line.

We think a lot about the game even before we walk on the practice field.

A player may kick the ball to score, or he may use his head, or any part of his body, but he may not use his hands or arms.

In a soccer game, there are 22 players on the field playing at the same time, 11 on each team, so, each team has eleven different positions. Each position is located at a different place on the soccer field, but of course you will leave your position when you need to. Each player has a special job to do to help his team score goals and also to help his team protect their own goal so the other team won't score.

The four main positions are the forwards, the halfbacks (or midfielders), the fullbacks and a goalie. The main job of the forwards is to score the goals for their team. The main job of the halfbacks is to help the forwards score by getting the ball and passing it to the forwards and help the defense by getting the ball away from the other team's attackers. The halfbacks also help the fullbacks. The fullbacks' main job is to stop the other team from scoring. The goalie is the last line of defense. His job is to keep the ball from going into the goal when the other team shoots it. He is the only player on the field who is allowed to use his hands or arms to catch the ball or block it. Your whole team works together both to score and to defend. When your goalie gets the ball, he starts the attack by kicking it or throwing it to your halfbacks or fullbacks. They, in turn, pass the ball to your forwards who are running down the field. The forwards pass the ball to one another until one is in a position to shoot, and hopefully score.

On defense, when the other team gets the ball, your forwards chase the ball carrier and some of the possible receivers down the field trying to get the ball away from them. If the other team passes the ball, one or more of your players should be close enough to any possible receiver to intercept the ball. If the other team dribbles by your halfbacks, your fullbacks try to take the ball away from them. If your fullbacks get the ball, they then kick it up to your halfbacks or forwards and start another attack. If the other team shoots at your goal, the goalie tries to stop the ball from scoring by hitting it or catching it.

DEAR MOM & DAD

I really like it when you come to my games. You cheer me on and give me somebody to play for. This way when we get home we can talk about all the different things that have happened in the game. And sometimes I can tell you how I feel about things.

I know it's tempting for you to yell at the referees. But before you do, please learn some of the rules first. Like offside.

The "Offside" is a simple rule but it is also very, very tricky. It wrecks the fun of the game when parents yell, "Offsides, offsides," at the players and the referee, especially when they're wrong.

I am just ahead of the next-to-last defender, (or am I) but you must remember: "Where was I when the ball was played?"

First, you can't be offside if you got the ball directly from a corner kick, goal kick, throw-in or drop-ball or from a player on the other team. To be offside, you have to be closer to the other team's goal than the ball is. Just at the instant the ball is kicked or headed by somebody on my team, look at me, and look at all the other forwards on my team. If any of us are in front of the ball, we are in an offside position. But, this doesn't mean that we're offside, since there is more to the offside rule than just that.

If we are in our own half of the field, we cannot be offside. If there are two guys from the other team between us and their own goal line, we cannot be off side. If one of us is in an offside position it's still not offside unless we are trying to take advantage of our position. If the ball is passed toward me or one of my teammates or if we distract or interfere with the defense, then the referee will blow his whistle and call us offside.

Some fullbacks know the rule real well and will try to put us offside. When they do that you may hear our coach remind us to stay awake. Sometimes things are very close and it is really difficult to tell from the sidelines if we were really offside.

Sometimes the referee makes a bad call. If he makes a bad call on me, don't feel too bad about it, because I'll feel bad enough for all of us.

Another rule that most parents get confused about is a hand ball. A hand ball is when the ball hits any part of your arm down to your hand. A hand ball has to be intentional, like when the ball hits an outstretched arm. If the ball hits the opposing team player's arm but the ball is in good position for your team, most likely the referee won't call a hand ball.

Hand Ball?!
That hit my arm!

Hand Ball!

All This too!

IN SOCCER All This, is considered part of your hand!

Part Two
THINGS CALLED SKILLS

Point the toe straight down to the ground for the instep drive.

THE INSTEP DRIVE
Kicking For Distance With Strength

An instep drive is a hard, low shot, usually at the goal. It is called an instep drive because it is a kick that is taken with the instep. (The instep is the part of your foot that your shoelaces cover.) The instep is a hard, bony surface that forms the top of the foot from the ankle to the base of the toes. The instep is the hardest part of your foot.

The purpose of the instep drive is to kick the ball hard and low, straight to the target. To do this, your instep must make contact with the center of the ball.

Steve shows the correct form for the instep drive. Notice where the non-kicking foot is planted.

Hit it below the center, and the ball will rise. If you hit the ball on the side, then it will curve and go the wrong way.

To make an instep drive, point your foot straight down, press your toes back, and raise your heel. This places your instep so it will be the first part to make contact with the ball.

Place your other foot along side the ball, about six inches away, with the toes pointing to where you want to kick it. Bend your knee slightly and push forward so that it is over the foot, and in line with the ball.

27

To keep the ball low when you kick an instep drive, lean forward over the ball as you kick. Your head should be in front of the ball, and the knee of your kicking leg should be directly over the ball when it's kicked. This may sound hard, but you'll get it!

First practice this kick with a still ball. Take a short unhurried run of about 4 or 5 steps before placing your supporting leg alongside the ball. When you kick, kick with a smooth swing of your kicking leg, and follow through in line with the path of the ball. Keep your arms spread apart to help you keep your balance.

You'll get lots of people telling you how to kick. The instep is the place covered by the shoelaces.

The fuller the knee action on your kicking leg, the faster the ball will go. Bend your knee back as much as you can before you take the kick, then sharply straighten it as contact with the ball is made.

If you are uncomfortable running straight on toward the ball on an instep drive, or if you keep kicking the ground, you can approach the ball from a slight angle. As you arrive at the ball, place your non-kicking foot about 6 inches away from it, with your toes pointing to where you want to kick it. Bend your knee a little bit and lean slightly sideways away from the ball. Point your kicking foot down and slightly outwards. Now, with the knee of your kicking foot over the ball, kick it with your instep.

SHOOTING
"What Soccer Should Be All About"

Shooting is the most important thing you can do in soccer. You have to shoot to score goals, and scoring goals is what helps your team win games. When you shoot, you must shoot accurately so you have a better chance of scoring. Try to shoot to where the goalie isn't and into the corner. The better you can shoot, the better chance your team has of winning.

You've got to want to score when you are near goal. Kenny shoots with the left foot.

Power kicking at the goal is just about as important as accuracy. If you kick a ball at the goal accurately, but with no power, the goalie can save it easy. If you can power kick the ball with no accuracy, the goalie won't need to dive to save the ball, as you will either kick it right to him, or wildly out of bounds. To be a good shooter, you need both power and accuracy.

lean
head
forward
over ball.

Practice this with a still ball, then a ball rolling away from you, like you are dribbling. When you do this you will have to place your non-kicking foot a little in front of the ball so that when you kick it, it will have rolled up in the right position.

To develop a strong and accurate kick, find a high solid wall that you can kick against. Place a mark on the wall by taking two pieces of masking tape and forming a cross. Then place the ball about ten feet away from the wall and kick at the cross. Every day try twenty kicks with each foot. When you get accurate, move to fifteen feet away, then to twenty feet away, then to twenty-five feet, and so forth. It is also very important to learn how to kick a bouncing ball. To do this you should throw the ball up in the air or against the wall and run on it and try to hit it at your target. If you practice these skills, you will be able to master both passing and shooting.

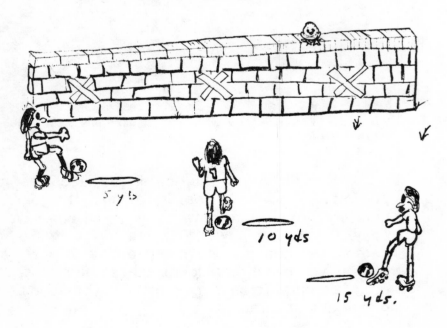

5 yds

10 yds

15 yds.

HEADING THE BALL

Heading is an important skill that you should learn. Heading will let you stop the ball when the other team kicks the ball high to their forwards or when they shoot towards your goal. It also lets you change the direction of the ball and make a quick pass to one of your team-mates. Lots of players don't like to head the ball when they should, so it goes past them. If they trap it and bring it down to their feet, the other team will often take the ball away from them.

Ken heads wide of the goal post during a league game.

To head the ball, keep your eyes open and your mouth closed and hit the ball with your forehead. Do not let the ball hit you or it will hurt. You hit it! Do not head the ball if it is under your waist or you might get kicked by another player. You can either head the ball to another player on your team or head the ball into the goal.

When we taught a friend how to head, we took a little piece of tape, put a little cross on it, and put it right in the middle of his forehead.

We took a light beachball and threw it up in the air and told him to hit the ball with the cross on the tape. As he got better in heading, we started moving to harder balls until we reached the regulation sized ball. We wanted to start easy because a bad first experience might have made him afraid of heading the ball for a while.

Now, sometimes we head a tether-ball back and forth to practice our

Oops, we forgot this time mouths should be closed.

heading, or we will hang a ball from a tree with rope or string over our heads to practice jumping up high and heading balls.

HEAD TRAP

The head trap is used on falling balls about head height. If there is nobody on your team near you, instead of heading the ball to no one, you can trap it and play the ball yourself. The forehead is used to make this trap. Adjust the angle of your head according to the flight of the ball so the ball hits the middle of your forehead. The steeper the drop, the more your head should be tilted back.

Tighten your muscles. Bend your knees slightly. Place one foot slightly in back of the other, about shoulder length apart. Watch the ball all the way to your forehead. As the ball hits, bend your front knee, so your whole body is lowered. This is to cushion the ball so it bounces upwards a little then falls right in front of you and you are ready for your next move.

Practice this trap a lot, because it is difficult to do. You can practice this by yourself by throwing the ball straight up in the air and trapping it. Also, get a friend to throw the ball to you so you get practice trapping it at different angles. Practice running to where the ball will drop. Quickly plant yourself, trap it, and run again with the ball at your feet. We think this is the hardest kind of a trap in soccer.

Lindy in a heading drill. After she heads it back to Steve, Kenny will throw her another ball.

PASSING

"It Links Your Team Together Like A Web"

Passing is one of the most important skills in soccer. It's an individual skill as well as a team skill. Passing lets you get past the defense without having to dribble and taking a chance of getting the ball taken away. Passing can put you into a position from which your team can score.

Before you can make a good pass it's important to learn where you want the ball to go, and why. You should also learn where to move to receive a pass when some other player on your team has the ball. (Called "moving off" the ball)

Lindy is getting open for a pass, even though she was behind Kenny.

I'm open

I'm being covered

Since getting into position to receive a pass is probably easier than making an accurate pass, we'll talk about that first. Also, knowing where you should be when your teammate has the ball will help you learn where you should make the pass when you have the ball.

When a member of your team has the ball, you should move to a position where he has the best angle to pass the ball to you. This means that you don't want to be behind a defender, because if you are behind a defender your teammate can't pass to you. If he tries, the opponent can intercept the ball by sticking his foot out or by heading it or by running and beating you to the ball.

You also don't want to be too close to your teammate when he has the ball. If you are too close, then passing to you doesn't do any good. The pass won't move the ball very far and one player from the other team can guard both of you.

34

Ways Of Passing

There are many different ways to pass the ball, but the most important and most accurate pass is the inside-of-the-foot pass. It is often called the "push-pass."

To make the inside-of-the-foot pass, you have to put the foot that you aren't kicking with by the side of the ball (about four inches away). Point your toes in the direction you want the ball to go. Bend your knee a little. Kick the ball with the large flat part of the inside of your other foot. This foot is like a golf club. It points directly out so the inside of the foot is forward. Raise it off the ground so it is even with the center of the ball. This is to keep the ball on the ground. Now, swing your foot forward so it hits the ball in the center and follow through in a straight line. To follow through means to kick right through the ball as if it wasn't there. Keep your foot swinging until your leg won't go any higher.

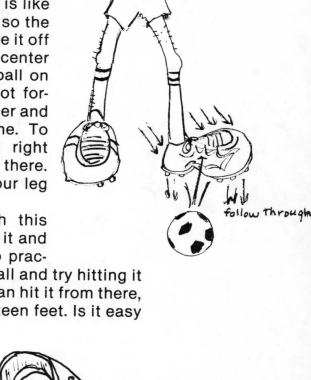

follow through

You will have trouble with this pass at first, but keep practicing it and soon your pass will be good. To practice this kick, put a target on a wall and try hitting it from about 5 feet out. After you can hit it from there, move back to ten feet, then to fifteen feet. Is it easy now?

Practice this drill both with a still ball and with a moving ball. Get someone to roll the ball to you from different angles and try to hit the target. Have someone roll the ball from behind you and chase the ball and try to hit it. Then dribble and try to pass the ball into the target. Have somebody throw the ball in the air, then you trap it and kick it back to him or to somebody else. Have somebody start even with you, then have him run down the field. Practice putting your passes in front of him so that he doesn't have to stop or run back for the ball.

Passing With The Outside

toe pointing
down

Another kind of push pass is the outside-of-the-foot pass. To make this pass, place the foot you are not kicking with by the side of the ball (about 6 to 10 inches away from it). The inside of your non-kicking foot should face to where you want to kick the ball, not like the inside-of-the-foot pass. You kick the ball with the outside edge of your other foot, right below your little toe. Your foot should be pointing slightly down and in toward your other foot. Keep your ankle stiff. Raise your other foot off the ground so it is even with the center of the ball. Now to kick the ball swing with the lower part of your leg, the part below your knee.

Practice the same drills as you do for the inside-of-the-foot push pass.

Both of these passes are not made for power but for accuracy, so don't worry if you can't kick the ball very far.

Now that you have learned the two most important kinds of passes, you can learn how to make harder and trickier passes.

WALL PASS

The wall pass is both a pass and a play. The wall pass is a quick exchange of passes by which two attackers can move the ball past a defender. The wall pass is used to get closer to a scoring position. This pass is named the "wall pass" because it reminds people of a ball being kicked at an angle against a wall and then bouncing back again, at an angle.

Wall passes aren't possible when players bunch up too much on the field.

As an attacker approaches the defender, he passes to his teammate who is next to, but a bit away from, the defender. The attacker continues to run forward past the defender. At the same time, his teammate passes the ball on the other side of the defender back to the first attacker who by this time has run forward past the defender. When this play is performed correctly, the wall pass can be a very threatening move to the other team.

The pass by the first player can be an outside or inside-of-the-foot pass. The first attacker should pass the ball as the defender starts coming close to him. The second attacker then passes the ball with the inside of his foot. If possible, he does not trap the ball. If he has to trap the ball, then he must pass it back fast. He should pass the ball to the open space behind the defender and in front of the first attacker.

WALL PASS

The first attacker should run around the defender and receive the ball without stopping or breaking his running stride. The ball should be passed so smoothly from first attacker to the second attacker and then back to first attacker so that the movement of both attackers and the ball appears continuous.

PACING PASSES

When your team is passing, you and your teammates should be moving around looking for open space. When you're running with the ball, your teammates should be running also. If, when you pass the ball, you try to pass it to where a teammate currently is, the ball will go behind him, and he won't be able to get it. Thus, you must pass the ball to where your teammate will be as he runs. This is called "pacing a pass."

Come on, move into that open space!! It's always there!

You must pass the ball so that your teammate can get possession of the ball and control it, without having difficulty and without slowing down.

A good way to practice pacing your passes is by forming two teams of about three or four players to play a "keep away" game. In "keep away", each team passes the ball around trying not to let the other team get possession of it. The first team to complete five passes in a row without the other team touching it wins. Everyone on your team should be moving around to open space so that they are in position to receive a pass. As soon as you pass the ball, move into open space so you can receive a return pass. If neither team can get five passes, make it easier for them by giving them one of your players.

Practice this skill often, and you can use this skill in your games. Always remember to move into open space and to pace your passes. Also you and your teammates should talk to each other so all of you will know when the pass will be made, where the ball is going to be passed to, and where the potential receivers should move to receive a pass.

SOLE-OF-THE-FOOT TRAP

The sole-of-the-foot trap can be used to control rolling balls, bouncing balls, or a high-kicked ball. To make this trap, the ball is stopped between the bottom of your foot and the ground.

When you use this trap, face the path of the ball, and crouch your body slightly.

Your weight is on your non-trapping leg. Place your non-trapping leg a little to the side of the path from where the ball is coming, and point it towards the ball. Also, bend your knee slightly.

Place your trapping leg about a foot in front of you and bend it a little. Point your toe up with your heel about four inches off the ground, your toes pointing up. Hold your arms out from your side to help keep your balance.

On a rolling ball, as the ball comes to you, get ready for the trap. As soon as the sole of your foot and ball make contact, shift your weight to the trapping leg and wedge the ball between the sole of your foot and the ground. Do this by rotating your foot forward and downward from your ankle so your foot is on the upper half of the ball facing you. Don't put your foot directly on top of the ball because you might lose balance and step over the ball. Now you are ready for your next move. What will it be?

THE-INSIDE-OF-THE-FOOT TRAP

To make an inside-of-the-foot trap, face your body towards the ball. Point your non-trapping foot toward the ball so that when the ball comes it rolls right by the inside of it. Face the inside of your trapping foot towards the ball. Stand so your heels are a couple of inches away from each other. Lean slightly forward. Raise your trapping leg and bend your knee slightly. Lift your foot so it is even with the middle of the ball. Let the ball hit the inside of your foot between your toes and your ankle.

When the ball hits your foot, immediately move your leg back, not up, keeping the inside of your foot in the same position. This cushions the ball so it won't bounce away from you. If the ball gets kicked to you hard, pull your leg back faster and sharper. Another way to help stop a fast moving ball is to stick your trapping foot in front of your other foot, still even with the center of the ball, so you can pull it back even farther for more cushion.

Most balls can be stopped with just a light touch. They should bounce about 12 inches in front of you so you can make your next move. From this position you can dribble the ball, pass it, or shoot it.

This trap can be made from a rolling ball on the ground or from a ball that is in the air. Remember, you have to get your foot even with the center of the ball. If your foot is too high, the ball will roll under it. If your foot is too low, the ball will bounce over it.

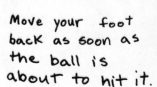

Move your foot back as soon as the ball is about to hit it.

OUTSIDE-OF-THE-FOOT TRAP

The outside-of-the-foot trap can be used to trap ground balls and bouncing balls. The outside of your foot, between your little toe and your ankle, is used to make this trap.

To trap a ground ball, line up to where the ball is rolling. Place your non-trapping foot sideways so your toe is pointing slightly outwards and the inside of your foot is facing the ball. Bend your leg a little.

If you can trap with the outside of the foot, you can do many more things with the ball . . . and quicker!

Your trapping foot is off the ground, slightly in front of your other foot. Point your foot inwards and downwards from your ankle. Lock your foot in this position. Now the side of your little toe is facing the ball. As the ball rolls to you, get ready and watch it all the way to the trap. As soon as the ball makes contact with your foot, move your lower leg slightly in front of you. Now you are ready for your next move.

To trap a bouncing ball, you trap it right after it bounces. Place your non-trapping foot on the ground with the inside facing the ball. Your trapping foot is pointed down and in and is locked at the ankle. Lift it over your non-trapping foot and slightly out in front. As soon as the ball bounces, swing your leg across your body and hit the ball with the outside of your foot. The ball should land slightly to the side of you. Now you are ready for your next move.

42

Chest Trap

The chest trap is probably the second most popular trap in soccer. It is used to control high kicked or high bouncing balls.

There are two kinds of chest traps. For both ways, the middle of your chest just above your stomach is used. This chest trap is for high balls: To make the chest trap, you should have your feet even with each other about shoulder's length apart, your knees bent, and your body leaning slightly back from your waist up. As the ball comes toward you,

Lindy traps a high ball during a game.

lean further back and spread your arms wide. This helps stretch your chest out more and helps you keep your balance. This also makes sure that you don't handle the ball. When the ball comes, take a deep breath and as soon as the ball comes, let your breath out to get extra cushioning. The ball should bounce off your chest to your feet so you can make your next move. What will it be?

The other kind of chest trap is for bouncing balls or balls coming upward at your chest. For this trap, place your feet even with each other, about shoulder's width apart. Lean your body from your waist up, slightly forward. Keep your arms out. When the ball comes toward you, lean forward a little more and put your chest into the ball. This is almost like the motion for heading the ball except you let the ball hit your chest. The ball will fall right in front of you so you're ready for your next move.

as ball hits chest, lean forwards

When you start doing the chest trap, you will probably be afraid of getting your chest in front of the ball. This is normal, so don't worry. Have somebody just toss the ball lightly to you from about five feet away. Try not to close your eyes. As you get good at this, have them toss the ball from farther back. Then have them start throwing a little harder, then still a little harder. Pretty soon you'll be able to chest trap a ball that has been kicked.

Sometimes you might want to jump for a chest trap.

Another problem habit you may develop when you start chest trapping is putting your hands in the way of the ball when it comes. To overcome this habit, hold a small rock or something like that in each hand to remind you not to move your hands in the way of the ball.

THIGH TRAP

The thigh trap is used to trap falling balls in the air. To make a thigh trap, you use the flat part of your upper leg. The part of your leg above your knee is used. When the ball comes, face the flight of it, and raise your trapping leg toward the ball.

How high you raise your leg depends on how fast the ball is coming, but never lift your leg above your waist. Bend your knee so your lower leg is pointing down. Relax your muscles. Don't flex them. As the ball hits your thigh, draw your leg back to cushion it. Your relaxed muscles will also help to cushion the ball. Now the ball should bounce lightly up and then be allowed to drop to the ground. When the trap is made, you're ready for your next move. What will it be?

Think of your thigh as a big soft cushion. It's the softest part of your "soccer body".

If the ball comes to you and is lower than you expect, just bend the knee of your non-trapping leg a little and raise your trapping thigh just slightly. As the ball hits your thigh, move your leg backwards to cushion it. This way when the ball hits you, it will bounce slightly forward, instead of bouncing up.

TRAPPING ON THE RUN

After you have practiced and learned these different kinds of traps in drills, you should try to do them on the run.

When you do these traps on the run, cushioning the ball is no longer a matter of withdrawing the part of your body that contacts the ball: it is a matter of controlling the ball's forward movement so it will bounce ahead of you and you can keep running. Be careful not to let the ball bounce too far in front of you, because then you'll lose it.

Sometimes the ball comes from strange places and you have to trap it any way you can.

As you trap the ball keep running with as little interruption as possible. If you don't push the ball enough ahead of you, you will stumble over it and lose control.

How close or how far you can let the ball bounce after a trap depends on the situation you are in. If there are no defenders around you, you can let it bounce farther out then if one is right on you.

Also when you are trapping on the run, you will have to quickly decide which trap you will use, depending on where the other team is, where your team is and on what position you are in.

For example, if you are running hard to receive a low ball coming from your left, you may have to trap it with the outside of your left foot, but if your weight is already on your left foot, you will have to make the trap with the inside of your right foot.

To practice all these traps, run up and down the field, throwing the ball in the air and trapping it when it comes down. Use all these different ways to trap the ball. First use the foot, then use the thighs, and so forth.

You can throw the ball up to yourself but it is better to have a friend throw it up for you. Then both you and he can run down the field throwing the ball up for each other. After you trap it, pick it up and throw it to your friend, then he traps it and picks it up and throws it to you.

BEFORE AND AFTER

If you trap the ball when an opponent is near, chances are that he'll take the ball away from you before you get to touch it again. To be able to trap the ball and beat the opponent, you must deceive the opponent. Make him go one way, then you go the other.

How do you deceive an opponent when you trap the ball? To do this, as the ball is approaching, you can move your body quickly in one direction, then suddenly the other way to trap the ball. This may throw your opponent off balance and give you extra time to play the ball and more space in which to move.

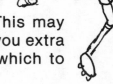

Another way is to change your direction and the direction of the ball right after you trap it. In other words, if you want to go to your left, turn so you would be going right. As the ball hits the ground after you trap it, turn towards your left on your left foot. As you do this, hit the ball with your right foot in the direction you are going and you are off.

If you are going to trap the ball with your foot, a good move is to swing your leg over it one way then trap it in a different direction and take off.

To do this, as the ball drops, swing the inside of your leg over the ball. As the ball bounces, trap it to the side with the outside of the same foot.

These are a few ideas of how to beat your opponent when you trap the ball. Practice doing this with a friend. Have him stand about six feet away and throw you balls to trap. As you trap the ball, have him run in on you and try to get the ball away from you. Do your fakes and he shouldn't get the ball. Practice this a lot. Try making up your own fakes, too.

Dribbling
"Being A Team Player While Keeping The Ball"

Steve in full control of the ball, while dribbling.

Finally you're in the play. You have the ball. Now, what do you do? You can either kick it, pass it, or dribble it.

What is dribbling? Dribbling is running with the ball while moving it with your feet. **Why** do you dribble? You dribble to move the ball down the field and to get away from someone. **When** do you dribble? You dribble when nobody is on you. Also, you can dribble to get by a defender when there is nobody to pass to. **How** do you dribble? To dribble, you run with the ball, moving it forward with a lot of little kicks. You must keep the ball close to you. If you kick the ball too hard, it will go too far in front of you and your opponent can kick it away. If you don't kick the ball hard enough, you won't be able to run very fast and you might trip over the ball and lose it.

There are two ways to dribble the ball. You can either use the inside or the outside of your foot. For both ways you hit the ball with your foot just under the center of the ball.

For inside of the foot dribbling, you use the area on the side of your big toe.

When you dribble with the outside of your foot, kick it just below the side of your little toe.

When you dribble, kick the ball with soft, delicate touches, just hard enough so you can run comfortably and not have to worry about the ball getting away from you.

To dribble, make short passes forward and run while doing it.

First, practice dribbling in a straight line for about 15 to 20 yards, until you get a running rhythm and you can hit the ball every other stride. (As you get better you should begin to run faster.)

Then you should try dribbling at a normal pace, then accelerate suddenly, then slow down, then accelerate again, so you get used to rapid changes in your own running pace.

When you are dribbling and a defender starts coming to charge you, pass the ball to a teammate. But, if a teammate isn't around, you must try to dribble around your opponent.

Dribbling slowly at first then accelerating is a good way of getting by opponents. The sudden changes in your speed will throw the other player off his timing. When you're dribbling and then have a sudden burst of acceleration you gain a few extra steps and a little extra space to do your next move, like shooting or passing.

When you dribble, look around for teammates and for opponents.

If you are dribbling fast with an opponent running alongside you, you can put your foot over the ball and come to a sudden stop. Your opponent will probably not be expecting that and will probably run on past you about three steps. Then you can move the ball in a different direction. This will give you more space to pass.

Another way to fool an opponent is by changing your direction suddenly. The trick here is to make your opponent think you will go in a different direction from the one that you intend. If you want to cut to your right, you can make a feint to your left, then as your opponent approaches, make an exaggerated step to the left. Flex your left leg and throw your body weight over it. To make the fake really

50

convincing, drop your left shoulder, put your right arm out, and raise your right foot, as though you were to play the ball to the left. As your opponent moves or leans across to try and stop you, brace your left leg, pushing your body to the right and off you go.

If you practice this a lot, you will be able to fake opponents out a lot. You can also try this fake using your other foot and going in another direction.

When you're dribbling don't have your head down looking at the ball because you have to see where your opponents are and if they fall for your fake. Also, if you look down you won't be able to see if anybody on your team is open.

If you try looking up you won't be able to dribble because you won't be able to see the ball.

The best place to look is at the ground in front of you. The farther ahead you look the better it is, but it's only better if you can keep control of the ball. This will give you more time to do your fakes.

Ken has his foot over the ball in an attempt to fake Steve out.

Shielding the Ball

Another important part of dribbling is screening, that is using your body to shield the ball. If a defender is at your right trying to get the ball away from you, dribble with your left foot so your body is between him and the ball.

Is this what the coach meant by screening?

If you practice these skills and fakes, you will become a good dribbler. And as you get better, you can be creative and make up your own fakes, too.

But, no matter how good a dribbler you are, you shouldn't dribble too often or too long.

A player who always starts dribbling when he gets the ball will soon find himself getting the ball taken away from him because the opponents will be able to read him.

When you dribble past one opponent don't let your success carry you to try to dribble past another, then another. You should always be looking for a teammate to pass to.

Here's Luis Lopez (second from right) with his three brothers. Luis is the world champion ball juggler. His brother Isidro made the trip to Portland with Steve.

BALL JUGGLING

Ball juggling is an excellent way for you to develop your confidence in your ability to control the ball and to build up your skill in shifting the ball from one part of your body to another for trapping and passing. Keep in mind that while ball juggling can be fun for its own sake, it isn't a skill that is frequently used directly in game play. How many times a person can juggle a ball does not tell you how good a player that person is. Ball juggling is a way to help gain the feeling of the ball and the ability to control it.

When you ball juggle, compete against yourself. If you can only keep the ball up three or four times, don't get discouraged. Keep at it. Slowly build up the number of times you can juggle.

Vary your practice. One time, practice juggling only with your feet. The next time, only with your thighs or only with your head. Then mix them. Juggle a few times with your feet, then move the ball up to your thighs, then move the ball to your head. If you really get good at juggling, try using your shoulders. That's a real challange.

Occasionally, you'll be able to use this skill directly in a game, like kicking the ball up to your head to head it, or dropping the ball from your thigh to your foot to kick it. When you do this, the other team probably will be surprised, and you'll beat your opponent and may gain the extra few seconds that will help you to advance the ball into scoring position.

"You Always Must Be Aggressive"
Tackling

Go hard into the tackle by dropping your shoulder slightly. Which one of us is likely to get the ball?

Tackling, in soccer, is simply using your feet to take the ball away from an opposing player. First, before you try to steal the ball, you must think to yourself, "The ball is mine — I'm going to get it". If you think this way, then you have a better chance of getting the ball.

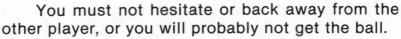

You must not hesitate or back away from the other player, or you will probably not get the ball.

As the dribbler comes towards you, crouch slightly and concentrate on the ball. Don't watch the player because he will try to fake you out. Move into tackle as soon as he hits the ball with his feet in his dribble. This is the time when he has the least control of the ball.

As he touches the ball, take a short step with one foot and plant it. Place the middle of the inside of your other foot securely against the middle of the ball. Put your weight forward. This will force the ball out from his feet and you'll come out with the ball.

To do this well takes a lot of practice. Practice doing this with a friend. Have him dribble the ball, and you stand in front and charge at him. Also practice running from behind him and getting in position to tackle him.

At first when you practice this, do it at half-speed so you get the idea. Then get faster and faster until you are at a normal pace.

SLIDE TACKLE

The slide tackle is a very difficult tackle to do correctly. This tackle should only be used in an emergency because once you've committed yourself, if you don't get the ball, the offensive player will go right by you while you're on the ground. If you're the last defender against the opposing team, the slide tackle is a very dangerous play. Also, do not do this tackle in the penalty area unless it is absolutely necessary, since a foul may give the opponent a penalty kick.

To make a sliding tackle, you must fall on the ground by sliding on your side. This slide is similar to the one a baseball player makes when sliding into a base. As you slide, one foot should hit the ball and force it out from the opponent's feet.

Do not be afraid of hitting the ground. Fall on the side of your leg closest to your opponent. Bend your outside arm slightly for balance. Swing your foot across to the ball, hitting it with the instep.

Slide tackles take a lot of practice. First practice sliding on the soft ground. Slide lightly at first, then work up your speed and force until you can do it harder. Once you get so you're not afraid of hitting the ground, practice doing slide tackles with a still ball. Then do it with a ball in front of a cone. As you get better at slide tackling, try and take the ball away from a friend.

I'm going to get it!

SHOULDER CHARGE

"Something You Seldom See"

The shoulder charge is the only legal way, in soccer, of purposely making another player lose his balance so that you can get the ball while he's dribbling.

The shoulder charge may be used when you are running alongside or catching up with an opponent. When you are running next to your opponent, adjust your stride with his while you lean against his side with your shoulder. Your arms must be at your side. Be careful not to stick your elbow out to the side or the referee may call a foul on you for pushing.

No one was ever hurt from a shoulder charge. Practice it. Remember the weight is on the outside foot.

Is this a fair shoulder charge by Steve? Why?

I got it all right!

Then, a final thrust is made. Your weight comes from your outside foot. Thus, lift your outside foot off the ground. Your inside leg should be bent. Put your weight towards the inside. Throughout this whole move, you should concentrate on both the ball and the player.

When your opponent is put off balance, you then have to run very fast to recover the ball. Once you have the ball, you may then turn with the ball and start a play. To practice shoulder charging, have a friend dribble the ball, and you use this move to try to take it away from him.

SHORT CHIP

The purpose of the short chip is to kick the ball over a defender's head, dropping it to your teammate on the other side of the defender.

To make the pass, place the foot you are not kicking with to the side of the ball about 6 inches behind it. Point it to where you want to kick it. Swing mostly with the lower part of your leg below your knee. Kick the ball with the top flat part of your foot, where your toes end, with a downward jab into the ground so your toes slide under the ball. There is no follow-through for this pass. The ball should rise steeply off the ground about 8 feet in the air, and it should have lots of backspin.

To learn the chip, have somebody roll the ball to you. Have your toes on the ground and your heel off. Let the ball roll up your foot. As the ball just gets on your foot, lift your foot in the air about 2 inches. The ball should come up about chest high. This drill will help you to get your foot under the ball. After you practice that, have the ball rolled to you and then make a chip pass. After you get good at that, practice making the chip pass over somebody's head from a still ball, or a ball rolling towards the receiver.

THE VOLLEY

A volley is any kick that is made when the ball is in the air. One kind of volley is the "front volley". This is the most straightforward of the volleys. This kick is just like an instep drive, except that it is done while the ball is in the air. To make this kick, face the ball. Place the leg that you aren't going to kick with so it will be alongside the ball, pointing to where the ball is aimed at the moment you kick it. A volley should be kicked as the ball is dropping when it's about 8 inches off the ground. To do this, raise your kicking leg at your hip joint. This limits the amount of backswing that your leg has. That's why the front volley is a kick made mainly from the knee. Swing from your knee with a short, sharp jab forward. When you kick the ball, lean forward with your knee and kicking leg over the ball. Once you do all this, you have done a front volley.

THE VOLLEY-(front)

leg raised at hip joint
while kicking knee is
bent over the ball

Non
Kicking foot
next to where the
ball will Land

SIDE VOLLEY

The front volley is a kick that is limited to balls that come in from a certain position. The side volley will allow you to kick balls that come in higher.

The side volley uses a completely different motion than the front volley. For most of the other kicks you had to place your supporting foot alongside and close to the ball, with your knee over the ball. For the side volley your non-kicking leg is placed much farther away. Place it about a leg's length away from the ball. Swing your kicking leg sideways at about a 45° angle to the ground, and fully stretch it when you kick the ball. To kick a side volley your instep is used. When kicking this volley, lean your body away from the ball. If you are kicking the ball with your right foot, you should be towards your left on your left foot, with your left foot about two feet away from the bouncing ball. As the ball comes, swing

58

your right leg sideways into it. Of all the soccer kicks, the side volley gives you the most leg swing.

At first when you try using this kick, only make a short leg swing and concentrate on your knee action. Make a sharp jab from the knee, with a downward chopping motion. Kick downward so you keep the ball low, since you don't want the ball just to fly wildly. Chopping down also helps to prevent hitting the ball with the outside of your foot, which then would spin it off, away from your target.

Here is a side volley, hit with the broad, flat side of the foot. This is used for short passes.

As you get good at the side volley, try turning your entire upper body into the ball as you kick it. This will put even more power into the ball when you kick it. But, you shouldn't try to do this until you can put the ball where you want it.

HALF VOLLEY

The half volley is a kick made immediately after the ball has bounced, no more than an inch off the ground. This kick is made with your toes pointing straight down. The ball is hit with the instep. The half volley is a tricky shot to keep low because when you kick it, the ball is already rising.

Place your non-kicking leg alongside the point where the ball is going to bounce. As you make the kick, remember to lean forward. Have the knee of your kicking leg slightly ahead of the ball as the kick is made. Swing your leg mostly from your knee, and have only a short follow-through.

To practice all of the volley kicks, have somebody throw the ball to you in the air. Use lots of balls, if you have them, and practice a long time. Take turns. Quickly decide which one of the three volley kicks you will have to use. Also, at first concentrate on timing the ball and judging where the ball is coming from and where it will bounce, because knowing where it will bounce is the main key for a successful volley.

Goalkeeping: A Special Job

The most unique position in soccer is that of the goalie. The goalie usually plays within the goalie box (goal area). The goalie is the only player on the soccer field allowed to use his hands and arms to play the ball within the field of play. He may only use his hands and arms within the penalty box. The goalie is the last player who can stop the opposing team from scoring. He has to block all the shots that are going under the crossbar and between the uprights. If he doesn't, then it's a goal for the other team.

The goalie may use his hands to catch the ball or to hit the ball away when the other team shoots the ball.

We take soft shots at Lindy from close range. This builds her confidence and teaches her to move and use her hands.

Many people think that blocking shots is the goalie's only job. But the goalie also starts offensive plays so your team can score. Also, a good goalie inspires the defenders and tells them where to position themselves. The goalie must be able to make quick decisions. These include: (1) Where to position himself, (2) Whether or not to attempt to take the ball away from an offensive player who has possession of the ball, and (3) Whether to play the ball or leave it for another player on his team.

GOALKEEPING: CATCHING THE BALL

The most important thing that every goalie must be able to do is be able to catch the ball without bobbling it. To be a good goalie, you must practice so that you will be able to catch the ball cleanly in any situation.

A GOALIE CATCH

The first thing you must remember is to watch the ball at all times. You must follow the ball's flight, right up to the moment when it is safely caught in your hands. Catch the ball so that your hands are slightly behind it. This will stop the ball from slipping through your fingers. Also, as you catch the ball, spread your fingers apart, your thumbs almost touching each other. Remember, if your hands are too far apart and if they aren't behind the ball, the ball might go right through your hands and into the goal.

When the ball is coming about head height, place your hands where the ball is heading for and relax your fingers and your wrists. As soon as you catch the ball, tighten your fingers up so you get a good grip on the ball, but your wrists should be still relaxed. This will soften the hardness and impact of the ball so it won't bounce away.

Whenever it is possible, try to get your body in front of the ball when you catch it. Just in case you miss the ball, the ball will hit your body instead of going into the goal.

If the ball is shot chest high, catch the ball against your chest. As it hits your chest, bring your arms around to catch the ball, so the ball is securely against your chest.

When you catch this kind of shot, the safest way to stand is with your feet planted on the ground about a shoulders-length apart. Your knees should be slightly flexed.

If the ball is bouncing up at you, lean forward over the ball and catch it, bringing it into your chest. This will give you plenty of body behind the ball in case the ball takes a bad bounce or in case you have somewhat misjudged it.

On ground balls, quickly get on one knee as you catch the ball. Catch the ball by scooping it up with your hands to your chest.

Sometimes, if a player dribbles in the penalty box and past your fullbacks, you must come out and grab the ball before he shoots.

We haven't played too much in goal, but it pays to practice the position. Lindy learns to use her hands and to "back up" the hands with the knee.

GOALIE: DIVING SAVE

If the ball is shot to a corner of the goal where you can't reach it, you must dive and try to catch it or you must deflect it so it doesn't go into the goal.

To dive after the ball, you push your body off the ground with the leg nearest the direction of your dive. Face your body towards the ball so your side is facing the ground. Fling your arms out towards the ball as both feet are lifted from the ground. The ball is caught with your arms outstretched.

Kenny holds the ball out, and Lindy grabs it, then falls to the ground. Goalie practice should be done in the soft grass.

As soon as the ball is caught, bring the ball into your chest. The ball and the forearm of your lower arm hit the ground first. At the same time, your other hand pushes the ball firmly down into the ground. As soon as you land, pull the ball into your chest.

This skill requires lots of practice because it is really hard to do. Start at first without the ball and take little dives so you get the technique and so you won't be afraid of hitting the ground. As you get better, increase the distance covered by your dives and practice with a ball.

If you cannot catch the ball because it is too far away for you to control, you can use your fist or open hand to punch the ball away. When you land, use your arms to break your fall. This may give the other team a corner kick but at least it isn't a goal.

GOALIE: Getting Rid of the Ball

In putting the ball back into play, you are allowed to take only four steps with the ball. In order to get the ball out the farthest distance, you can roll the ball to yourself out to the edge of the penalty box and kick it from there. When you roll the ball it only counts as one step because you are not holding it.

As you roll the ball, you are running right behind it. When you roll the ball, you must be careful not to let the other team take it away from you. If they start to charge the ball, pick it up. You may roll it again, around the opposition but you must be very careful.

When you stop rolling the ball, you have only a certain number of steps left to kick it. The number of steps you have left depends on how many times you rolled the ball. You should only roll it once or twice.  To throw the ball, hold the ball with your hand slightly underneath it. The same arm is drawn back and your elbow bent. Your other arm and your planted leg face the target. Now as your arm is thrown forward, your body should start to turn towards your target. As your turn is completed, the ball is released. As your arm swings, the ball should not go above head height. It should be released about a foot in front of your head.

To kick the ball, you should hold both hands under it with your arms out in front of you about waist high. Your elbows are slightly bent. Take a

step forward with your non-kicking leg. Swing your kicking foot up towards the ball. Keep your toes pointed. As your foot is swinging upward, move your hands out and drop the ball. The instep should hit the ball just as you drop it. The ball should go high and far. It takes a lot of practice to get the timing right, and to get the power for distance and to get control for direction.

You should also practice rolling the ball out with a friend trying to get it away from you.

The Angles of Goal Keeping

In order to be a better goalie, you must know how to cut off the angles of the goal when the ball is shot. You must know where the players are and where the ball is. If you do this, you will be able to save more shots.

How do you cut off the angles? When the opponent takes a shot from the center, the goalie should be in the center of the goal. This gives the other player the least chance to score because you have an equal chance at both sides of the goal to save the ball.

If the opponent takes a shot from a little to the side, the goalie should move a little bit to that side. You should move so, from where the shot is taken, there is equal distance on both sides of the goal where the ball could go.

You must practice a lot until you get the hang of where the position is that allows the least possible scoring.

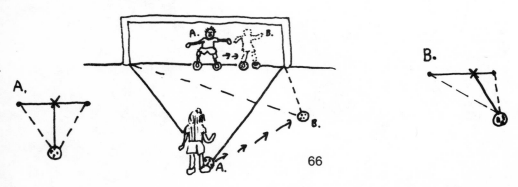

66

Kenny is on the goal line. He should come on out to "cut the angle".

To practice this just have somebody or a group of friends keep taking shots over and over while you try to get in position to save the ball. Do this over and over until it becomes instinct where you are supposed to stand when the ball is shot from a certain place. Also, shout to your fullbacks where to go if you see a possible shot. If your player moves there, this will help prevent the shot from being taken.

That's better, Kenny. What a difference 4 meters makes!

Part Three
RESTARTS: WHEN THE BALL IS NOT IN PLAY

Almost half of all goals scored develop directly from restarts. To gain an edge for your team, practice the quick throw-in.

THE KICK-OFF

The kick-off is the way that a team puts the ball into play at the start of each half and after each goal.

At the beginning of the game there is usually a coin toss. The winner gets his choice of kicking off or of defending the goal that he chooses.

KICK-OFF

BALL STARTS ON HALF-LINE

COIN TOSS DECIDES WHO KICKS OFF

On the kick-off, the ball is placed on the halfline in the center of the middle circle. Your whole team must be on the side of the halfline that they are defending. If you are kicking-off, then the other team must not only be in their half, they must also be outside the center circle.

After kicking, the first kicker may not touch the ball a second time until it is touched by another player. Also, the ball must move forward at least the distance of its circumference. Thus, the best thing to do is pass it. In one play, one forward passes the ball slightly forward to another forward who then can either pass the ball to an outside forward or back to a halfback. The other team will probably charge in to try to get the ball away from you, so you must do all these passes quickly. The halfback then can either kick the ball upfield or pass it to another player.

69

When the other team kicks-off, your forwards should be ready to run in from behind the circle. Before play can start with a kick-off, the referee must blow his whistle. However, you can't start to rush until the ball moves the distance of its circumference. Thus, as soon as the other team touches the ball, your team should be charging to try to get possession of it.

GOAL KICK

A goal kick is the way of putting the ball into play when it goes out of bounds across the goal line after last being touched by a player from the offensive team.

The ball may be placed anywhere inside the goal box as long as it is placed on the side where the ball went out. The ball must go out of the penalty area before being touched again or the goal kick must be taken over.

A fullback or goalie can either just kick the ball upfield or they can try various plays. One play is to kick the ball just outside of the penalty box to a teammate who then taps it back to the goalie. Then the goalie kicks the ball down the field. A fullback should cover the goal while the goalie comes out. While the goal kick is being taken, all of the other team's forwards should be covered by your halfbacks in case of a bad kick. The kicker should try to kick the ball towards the wings.

When you try the play, if the other team starts to cover the goalie after the fullback kicks the ball, then the fullback with the ball should just dribble it down the side of the field or kick it down the field. If necessary he should kick it out of bounds. The goalie should quickly get back into goal.

CORNER KICK

The corner kick is a special kind of free kick that is given to the attacking team when the defense touches the ball last, before the ball crosses the goal line. This kick is taken from within a one-yard arc in the corner of the field that is closest to the point where the ball went out.

When defending against a corner kick, the goalie should stand on the goal line and about three-fourths of the way back from the post closest to the ball. If the ball comes into the middle, the goalie should grab it. The reason the goalie should stay back is so he can run up on the ball if he needs to. It is much harder for the goalie to run back. One defensive fullback should stand against the near post so the ball can't go past it. He can just block the ball and get it out. One fullback should stand against the far post, so that if the ball is going into the goal, he can just put his body in front of it and kick it out. The rest of the fullbacks and halfbacks should cover the other teams' forwards and halfbacks in the middle.

When your team gets a corner kick, the other team will probably line up the same way. On a corner kick three forwards should line up in front of the goal, one just outside the far corner of the goalie box, one in the middle just outside the goalie box, and the third near the other corner of the goalie box. Your players should move around so that the other team can't easily cover you. Then as your teammate kicks the ball, your halfbacks should be lined up just inside the penalty box.

The kicker should try to kick the ball in the air toward the edge of the goalie box. Then the forwards can head the ball into the goal. If the ball bounces out, then your halfbacks can try and score. If the ball isn't in the air, you should just kick it.

Another corner-kick play is the "short" corner kick. Your team lines up in the same way, but a halfback or forward runs out quickly toward the kicker. The kicker immediately passes the ball to him. Then the kicker runs behind the other player to receive a pass from him. Then the original kicker can shoot, dribble then shoot, or he can center the ball.

Quick

If a defender follows and has the person who runs up covered, a second player on your team can run towards the kicker, or the kicker can just kick the ball across the middle like he would normally do. He should kick it while the defenders are still close to him so there are fewer defenders in the middle of the goal area. You should turn corner kicks into goals!

THE THROW-IN

Nearly every soccer player will take a throw-in sometime. Your team gets a throw-in when a player on the other team plays the ball past the touchline, and out of bounds. It is taken where the ball goes out. While the rules on throw-ins are a little technical, just remember a few things and you won't have any problems with the referees blowing their whistles and calling you for a foul throw-in.

The first thing to remember is to keep both your feet behind the touchline and on the ground. Take the ball with your hands slightly behind it and put both your hands straight over and behind your head. Now bring the ball back over and behind your head, then throw it. Both hands should throw the ball with equal force. The ball should not spin sideways.

If both feet are not on or behind the line, or if the ball isn't thrown from directly behind the head, the referee may blow the whistle and give the throw-in to the other team.

74

You may not throw the ball in to yourself. In other words, when you throw the ball in it has to touch another player either on your team or the other team before you can touch it again.

Where should you throw the ball? The throw-in is often an overlooked move in soccer. A throw-in gives your team possession of the ball. You can quickly start an attack on the other team's goal. If you get the ball real fast and take a throw-in before the other team has a chance to get ready, you have a big advantage. Your team can dribble down to the other team's goal and shoot, or they can quickly pass the ball to a breaking forward, or they can kick the ball across the field to the winger who should be wide open to score.

The throw-in is so easy. The biggest mistake in throw-ins is not throwing the ball in quickly.

When your team is taking a throw-in, your players shouldn't be standing waiting for the ball. They should be moving around trying to get open. One play is for a player to stand next to the thrower. As the thrower starts to throw the ball, the player runs down the wing. The thrower throws the ball just over the player's head. The ball will bounce in front of him and he has a break-away.

On this play, you don't have to worry about being off-side because on a throw-in you can't be off-side until a second player on your team plays the ball.

This is just one example of throw-in play. Your team can work out other plays, too.

If you practice throw-in plays, then a throw-in could be a very good scoring opportunity for your team.

THE FREE-KICK

A free kick is often an attack on goal. Why are these players standing around and watching?

A free-kick is a play-making opportunity which can lead to a goal.

On a free-kick your team gets a chance to kick the ball into play while the other team must stand back.

When the referee calls a free-kick, the ball is placed on the spot where the foul was committed. The other team has to stay at least ten yards away from the ball. They may not charge in on you until you have kicked the ball and it has moved its circumference (about two feet).

In a game, when you are given a free-kick, if any of the players on the other team don't get ten yards away, you may ask the referee to give you your "ten yards". He will then move them back, but you must wait.

When do you get a free-kick? When a player on the other team commits a foul or infraction. There are two different kinds of free-kicks: An "indirect free-kick" and a "direct free-kick".

When the referee blows his whistle and holds his arm up in the air, he is awarding an indirect free-kick. An indirect free-kick is called for dangerous play, obstructing an opponent, or for too many steps by the goalkeeper.

On an indirect free-kick, at least two players have to touch the ball before a goal counts.

On a foul like striking, kicking, tripping, jumping, charging violently, charging from behind, holding, pushing or a hand ball, the referee will blow his whistle. Your team then gets a direct free-kick. A direct free-kick means that you may kick the ball right into the goal and score without it touching another player.

FREE KICKS (Strategy)

If your team is given a free kick, you can either pass the ball to a teammate or just kick it. If your team gets a free kick near the other team's goal, you can either shoot at the goal or you can try a special play to score. Thus, it is important for your team to practice different plays to use on free kicks from different areas of the field.

When the other team has a free kick near your goal, four or five defenders should stand side by side in a line like a "wall" about ten yards away from the ball. This line should stand between the ball and the goal with the endman between the ball and one post. This is to block part of the goal. If they kick the ball to the part of the goal where the wall is, the wall will just block it. The goalie will position himself in the part of the goal that isn't blocked to cover that area. The halfbacks that are not in the wall should cover the other team's players so they can't pass the ball to them on the kick. This doesn't leave very many places for the other team to shoot at.

When your team has a free kick near the other team's goal, the other team will probably set up their defense in the same way. If you want to shoot the ball for a goal, you should chip it over the wall to the part of the goal that the goalie isn't covering.

This shot is very hard to do. Thus, your team might want to do a play that deceives the other team. One play is to have three players act as if they're going to take the shot. The first player runs up to the ball, steps over it and runs to the side. Right after the second player has started to run, the third player runs up and shoots the ball. This play can be done in less than five seconds, so it doesn't give the other team time to think. The ball should be shot into the very corner of the goal where the goalie is trying to block. After you do this play once, the next time you can let the second player or even the first player kick it. If you line up with three players, the other team might not expect a quick kick. This is only one kind of play. Your team can pass to the side and shoot. Or your team can shoot hard at the wall. Or you can make up your own plays or do variations on any of these plays.

Indirect free kicks are different. One play for an indirect free kick is to have a player stand with the ball on the ground between his feet. Another player, behind him, lightly taps the ball so it rolls in front of the first player. Then the first player runs up and shoots the ball. This play can also be done on a direct free kick. A free kick, especially one near the other team's goal is always a scoring opportunity. Here, surprise is most important, and practice can help your team score goals.

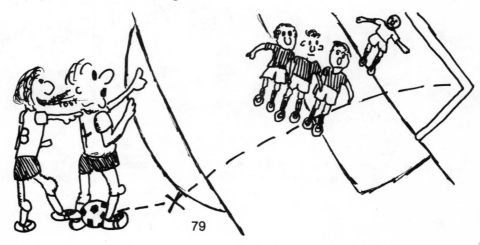

PENALTY KICKS

The penalty kick is one of the most dramatic single moments in soccer. A penalty kick is a free shot at the goal with nobody to beat but the goalie. If it is shot correctly, it should be an automatic goal every time.

A penalty kick is awarded if the defending team intentionally commits a foul in their own penalty box. These fouls are kicking, tripping, jumping at an opponent, charging from behind, charging violently, hitting, holding, pushing, or if a player, other than the goalie, hands the ball.

If the referee sees one of these fouls committed in the penalty box, he will blow his whistle and point to the penalty spot, awarding a penalty kick. The ball will set on the penalty spot, 12 yards away from the goal line. All the players have to be outside of the penalty box, except the kicker and the defending goalie. The players outside of the penalty box will be ready to rush in as soon as the ball is kicked. The goalie has to have both feet touching the goal line.

The penalty kicker should aim low in either corner. That's the hardest shot for the goalie to get.

If you are taking the penalty kick, the first thing you should do is forget about the yelling spectators. Think of something entirely different, until you are ready to take the kick. If you think of all the spectators yelling, you will get very nervous. If you start thinking about what will happpen if you miss, you probably will. Just imagine that you have a teammate in the corner of the goal behind the net. Then, try to pass the ball right to him.

If the referee puts the ball in a hole or in a place that you don't like, move it a couple of inches to the side where you do like and brush away any small pebbles that might affect your shot.

Then make your decision where you are going to kick the ball. After you make this decision, keep it, and don't change your mind. If you change your mind when you are about to kick it, you will most likely make a bad kick.

HINTS TO REMEMBER:

● When you make your decision, you should know where you are going to kick the ball. When the referee blows his whistle and you are ready to run up to shoot, just look at the ball. Don't look up at the goalie because he might be leaning to one side to try and make you suddenly change your mind. It doesn't matter if he is leaning to the side where you are kicking anyway, because it will still go in the corner and he won't have a chance.

● When you are running to kick the ball, just run normally like you would if you were passing the ball to someone. If you run one way then another way to try and fake out the goalie, you are most likely going to fake out yourself and miss the shot.

● When you shoot, try to get the ball in the lower corner of the goal. If you just try to kick it as hard as you can to the center of the goal, the goalie will probably save it every time. Try to shoot the ball within 5 feet of the post.

● The best way to take a penalty kick is to do it with the inside of your foot because that is the most accurate. The kick doesn't have to have tremendous force, as long as it's accurate.

● When you take a penalty kick you have to wait for the referee to blow his whistle. If the goalie moves before you kick it and you miss, the referee will give you the penalty kick over. If you score when the goalie moves too soon, it is still a goal. If one of the other team's players jumps into the penalty box before you shoot and you miss, you get the kick over. If you make it, it is still a goal. If your teammate jumps into the penalty box before you shoot and you miss, you miss. If you score, you have to take it over.

● When you shoot, if the ball hits the goal and bounces back, and the goalie doesn't touch it, you can't kick it again until a player from the other team or a teammate touches the ball. Then you are free to kick it. If you do touch it before someone else does, the other team gets a free kick.

● If you shoot and the ball bounces off the goalie, you can shoot right away.

When you first practice a penalty kick, practice kicking it different ways. Feel which way is most comfortable. When you find out which way is most comfortable to you, stick to that one way when you practice and in the games. When you get real good at penalty kicks, practice shooting for the other corner or with the other foot. But in the game only do what you are best at.

● A good way to practice either alone or with a goalie is to set on each side of the goal a corner flag or stick 3 feet away from the goal post. Set another flag 5 feet away from the goal post. Practice shooting between the sticks and goal posts. If you can shoot the ball between the stick 3 feet away and the stick 5 feet away, you most likely will score a goal. But if you can shoot the ball between the goal post and the stick 3 feet away, you will have a goal every time.

Why didn't I practice these when I had a chance?!

Part Four
PROBLEMS

The best place to deal with problems is on the practice field, instead of during a game.

WHAT TO DO WHEN THERE IS A
GLORY-HOG ON YOUR TEAM

There may be one on your team.

      Lots of teams have at least one glory-hog. A glory-hog isn't very much fun to have on a team because he wrecks the team spirit and ruins the team's play. Passing is the key to good team play and to scoring goals. One thing that a glory-hog won't do is pass the ball. When the hog has possession of the ball, he will dribble too much. Even if he is a good dribbler, there is no way that he'll be able to dribble through all of the other team. Most of the time the hog will lose possession of the ball. When the other team spots a ball hog, they'll double team him as soon as he gets the ball, or just wait until he gets tired.

Another thing a glory-hog will do is take lots and lots of bad shots at the goal. Often he is encouraged by the parents who shout, "Nice try!" and "Good shot!" They do this because the shot looks impressive, especially when it's a high shot that goes way over the goal. They really shouldn't encourage the glory-hog to take these kinds of shots, because every time he does he loses a chance for his team to score.

Sometimes it's hard to know whether a player is a glory-hog or if he just doesn't play well under pressure. This kind of player will take shots on goal when he should have crossed the ball to an open teammate. Sometimes he does cross the ball. However, usually the pass is bad.

One way of dealing with a glory-hog is not to pass the ball to him. The boys on the team find it is very tempting to "get even" this way. However, trying to "get even" soon wrecks the team's play. Talk to your coach and have him talk to the glory-hog. During the game, forget about him. Play the way you normally would.

HOW TO PLAY AGAINST SOMEONE
WHO IS TWICE YOUR SIZE

Look at these guys! They're all bigger than I am!

When you start out playing soccer, most of the guys you play against will be bigger than you. This can be quite scary. Both of us are very small. Therefore, nearly everyone we play against is bigger than we are. Thus we learned some tips which we will pass along to you.

When you are defending, just get in the way of the guy who has the ball. Then he'll either have to slow down or change his direction. This makes it harder for him to control the ball and easier for your teammates to get the ball away from him.

When he's dribbling, you should shoulder charge him and try to push him off the ball. If he's trying to keep control of the ball and you are pushing against him, it is tough for him to keep both his balance and his mind on what he's doing.

Practice having one-on-one drills with your team. Pretty soon you'll find yourself getting the ball away from them a fair share of times. This will help you build up your confidence. Another thing your coach might do is put you man-for-man on one of the other team's stars. Then your job is to stay close to him and get to the passes before he does. If he does get the ball, then you and another player on your team should try to take it away from him at the same time. If he has to watch out for both of you at the same time, he'll probably lose the ball or at least kick badly.

WHAT TO DO WHEN
THE OTHER GUY PLAYS DIRTY

A player nails me right in the knee with a sliding tackle.

Sooner or later when you play soccer you will run into someone who plays dirty. He might trip you, push you, kick your shins, or use his elbow and fist. He will usually try this in the middle of the field and when the referee isn't looking. He'll try it because most referees will be watching the play and won't see it. And even if the referee does see it, it won't hurt his team too much because all you'll get is a direct free kick from the middle of the field.

There really aren't too many things you can do about it. You can try telling the referee to watch out for him. Some referees won't listen to a player at all. Other referees will tell you that they will watch out, but most of the time they won't. Some referees will even bawl you out for talking to them. But sometimes a good referee will listen, and he'll really watch the kid playing dirty.

If you're playing in a neighborhood league where the parents on both teams know each other, then you might go over and ask the other coach in front of the parents of both teams to ask "Bobby" to stop kicking you. If enough boys from your team complain, maybe the other coach will do something about the dirty player.

The best thing you can do about this is to just stay away from the dirty player and just play your own game.

One other thing that might help is to wear shinguards. We wore shinguards when we first started playing. Then, when we got older, we stopped wearing them because one of our coaches thought they slowed us down. And we thought that they were uncomfortable. Now we wear them when we think the other team is going to be rough. We find that wearing shinguards is less uncomfortable than getting a really good kick in the shins. We feel that it is better to be safe than sorry!

You should know when and how to put shinguards on.

Part Five

STORIES

One of the greatest stories in all of soccer is about Pele. Here he is on his first visit to the United States.

THE BIG CONTEST

One day while my family and I were eating at a local restaurant we saw a sign that said, "There is going to be a National Soccer Skill Contest." The sign also said where and when it was going to be held.

On the day of the contest, Bob Evans, Coach of the South Bay Gunners, took my brother Kenny, our friend Brian, and me to the place where the contest was being held. There were two age categories, the under 10 years and the under 14 years. I was in the under 10. They tested us on accuracy with our left foot, and with our right foot. We also had to try to keep a ball in the air as long as we could, using all parts of our body except for our hands. They called this "ball juggling."

At the end of the contest we all came home and told our parents all about the contest.

About three days later I got a telephone call. It was from a man named Norm Nielsen. This is what he said in our conversation: "Hi, I'm with the California Youth Soccer Association. I looked over the scores of the contest and your's were the highest. You won." I ran upstairs and told my Mom and Dad that I had won the skills contest. They asked me who won for the under 14 group. I said, "A boy named Isidro."

L.A. AZTECS

I told my Mom the rest of what the man said: "Three days ago you won for Los Angeles and Orange Counties. Tomorrow you will have a chance to try to win the State Championship." I asked him where it would be held. He said that it would be held at the half-time of the Los Angeles Aztecs' soccer game. After I told my Mom this she said, "Then you had better get some sleep." So I went to bed.

The next morning I woke up at about 9:30. I ate breakfast and then put on my uniform and soccer shoes.

We left for the game at 11:00. When we got there, I saw Isidro warming up. I asked Isidro who we were going to run against. He said, "The winners of San Diego and the winners of Arizona."

A crowd started to fill the stands. That meant that the game would start soon.

It was about 25 minutes into the game when number 13, Uri Banhofer, of the Aztecs scored. About a minute later number 5 of the Portland Timbers scored on a breakaway. The referee blew his whistle. It was half time. Time for the big contest.

I was two out of two on my accuracy with my left foot, and one out of two with my right foot. I ball juggled for ten seconds. The ref told all of the boys in the contest to line up in the middle of the field because he was going to announce the winners of the contest. In his microphone he said, "The winner of California and Arizona in the under ten category is . . . . .Steve Laitin." He gave me a trophy and shook my hand. Then he said, "The winner of California and Arizona in the under 14 category is . . . . . Isidro Lopez." He gave him a trophy and shook his hand. He said in his microphone to the specators, "Steve Laitin and Isidro Lopez just won for the two states of California and Arizona in the National Youth Skills Contest. Steve and Isidro also win a free trip to Portland, Oregon".

MY TRIP TO PORTLAND
by Steve

On August 12, at about 1:30 my Dad and I met Isidro at the Los Angeles Airport.

Isidro and I each brought a camera, clothes for the next day, and a soccer ball. The airport was very crowded. Lots of people asked us where we were going, and what we were going to do. Everyone was very friendly. Soon a man announced our flight number. And it was time for us to get on the airplane.

The plane took off. Just after take-off the stewardess came around with drinks and peanuts. She told Isidro and me that we were too young to drink the wine, but she said we could have a soft drink if we wanted to. Soon after, she served us lunch. We had steak, chili, salad, cake and milk. The day was very clear, and we could see very far out the window. We saw Crater Lake and Mount Shasta.

It was nearly four o'clock when we landed in Portland. We got a taxi and went right to the hotel. We checked in. They gave us rooms 108 and 110. These rooms were very large. Each had two big double beds. The carpets were very thick. And they had a lot of nice pictures on the walls. Isidro had never been in a hotel before and was very thrilled. He must have bounced up and down on his bed nearly one hundred times. Then he said, "This place is swell. Let's go see what the rest of it looks like."

We walked around. They had a nice swimming pool with a sun deck; nearby was a miniature golf course and a restaurant. Their lobby was very big and had fountains.

We went back to our room and started to get ready for the soccer game that night. Soon the telephone rang. It was the man from the hotel telling us that the taxi to take us to the stadium was waiting for us in front of the hotel. Isidro, my Dad and I hurried to the front lobby. We were eager to begin the ride to the stadium.

AND 31,000 FANS CHEERED

When we got to the stadium it was almost empty. The only people who were there were the ushers, the people setting up in the concession stands, the groundkeepers, the players and us. Then they opened the gates and within a few minutes the stands were full. The sell-out crowd of 31,000 people filled every seat, and every possible standing space in the stadium. Also, at every nearby building, people were watching from roofs and windows.

The TV director explained to us how the cameras worked, and that we would be on TV! Soon we were dribbling, shooting and ball juggling. The fans were in a good mood and kept applauding us. After that there was still some time so we played a short game with the ballboys. The score was 0 to 0 with about one minute to go. The TV director waved the time to us. Just then the ball was passed to me. I trapped the ball, kicked it a little bit in front of me, and shot. The ball went high. The goalie leaped. The ball went past him, into the right top corner of the net. The crowd cheered! Time was up. Our game was over.

Now it was time for the playoff game between the Portland Timbers and the Seattle Sounders. Both teams were charged up for this important game. For seventy minutes both sides fought, but neither team was able to score. Suddenly there was a breakaway by Portland. The crowd screamed. The shot headed toward the lower right corner of the goal. The goalie dove — and saved it. The fans groaned. Before anyone could tell what was happening, the Seattle goalie threw the ball to his right halfback. The right halfback crossed it to the inside left. The inside left shot and the ball was in the net. The score was now Seattle 1 - Portland 0. The crowd gasped and groaned.

The Portland team was frantic! They fought hard, but Seattle stayed tough. Then, with about two minutes to go, Portland scored. The game ended in a tie and went into overtime.

Portland kicked off. Both teams were playing their hardest. The players took every possible shot for the goal. Then all of a sudden it was all over. Portland had won. The fans screamed and screamed. We congratulated the players and got their autographs.

Here's Civic Stadium in Portland, Oregon, where 31,000 cheered.

That night at the hotel we were all too excited to sleep. My Father spoke to the manager, and got permission to take us down to the parking lot. There we played soccer until 2:00 a.m.

Then we all went upstairs to sleep. Tomorrow was going to be another big day.

Oh, I forgot to tell you, I came in third in the competition.

Part Six
THINKING SERIOUSLY ABOUT SOCCER

Here are two teammates running after the same ball — too much teamwork! That's Ken with the head band.

WORKING TOGETHER AS A TEAM

In order for your team to work well together, you have to have each player feel good about himself as an individual. The players also have to feel good about each other and about the team as a whole. You cannot have any stars, or glory hogs on the team, and everyone on the team has to be in good shape and be able to run constantly for the whole game. If your team meets these standards, then they are on their first step in becoming a good team that works well together.

If a team works well together, then whenever a player gets the ball, he knows that the rest of his team will be moving into open space to help him move the ball down the field. He also knows that there are other players who will be backing him up so he doesn't have to worry as much about losing the ball.

Decisions! Decisions!

When a player on your team gets the ball, think about what you should do. Should you move to the touchline to spread out the defense? Should you break forward? Should you move to open space where he can easily kick the ball to you? You have to use your own **good** judgment. Look at the situation, read the play and see what is needed of you! If you are in a tight area, it might be better if you ran down the field and took a defender with you, so the player on your team with the ball would have more space to use. But if your teammate only has one or two defenders to beat, then it might be better to run towards him, into an open space where he can get the ball to you.

You have to practice moving into open space. You have to practice covering up for other people. You have to constantly work at reading the plays before it will become a habit. But when these actions become instinctive, you will find that you will be an improved player and that your team will be working well together and will be winning games.

An Idea for Great Field Positioning

On the field there are three possible situations: your team has possession of the ball, the other team has possession of the ball, or the ball is being fought over. In each of these cases, you must constantly think: Where should I go? What should I do?

We got a lot of practice in making decisions by having our coach walk around the field with the ball. He would have us position ourselves based on the situation he described. Soon we were able to position and re-position ourselves very quickly during games. Since most coaches do not pay much attention to this type of drill, it would be a good idea if

you asked your coach to do this drill several times with you. Since every coach has his own ideas about exactly what you should do in each position, there is no good way for you to learn what is expected of you unless you ask him to tell you clearly, exactly what he expects. Also, with this drill everyone on the team can learn what everyone else on the team should be doing in various situations. Thus, this drill helps the players to give instructions to each other as the game develops.

General Ideas on Tactics

As your team gains experience playing together, ideas on tactics will develop. At first your team should try simple moves to get past the other team. If some plays work, you should keep practicing them and use them in games.

For example, if your halfback or wing has the ball on one side of the field, the other team will move mostly towards the same side of the field. Then your halfback can pass it to a wing or another halfback on the other side of the field. Your player now with the ball should have an open field ahead of him because the opposing team now has to shift back to the other side of the field. This takes time because suddenly their attention is shifted, and they have to mark different players.

Another play is: If a winger has the ball, an inside should start to run down the wing. As soon as he starts breaking, the winger should pass the ball down the wing to the open space and run into the middle to take the inside spot. The inside forward will be running toward the open space. He will then receive the ball and should have an open field ahead. The inside forwards can also do this play in the middle of the field near the goal. As soon as the pass is received, a shot on goal can be taken.

Using Triangles

Also, your team should always run and pass in triangles. This is so a player will always have someone to receive the pass. A triangle means there should always be two players in position near the person with the ball so he can pass it to one of them. You can work the ball up the field with triangles. When the ball is passed, a new triangle should be formed with the person now carrying the ball.

When you run and pass in triangles, you must get rid of the ball fast. Here's an exercise for you: Steve's in the middle, receiving quick passes first from me, then from Lindy.

The triangle is formed with two people in front and with a backup man. This man is known as the "support man". If the other team intercepts the ball from one of the front players, there is a man in back of them to stop the opponent. Also you should generally pass forward. The two front men can work forward with the ball with each other and if they get into trouble or are covered, then they can pass the ball back to their support. If the two men are in back and pass the ball to each other, and if it's intercepted, there is no one backing them up and the other team could get a breakaway. When a ball is passed back to the support man, there should be a player next to him to pass to, and a support player in back of him.

THEY didn't work in triangles, so I stole the ball!

Triangles should also be used on defense. If the fullbacks are lined up, in a straight line, then a pass can go past all of them and they are all beaten. If one fullback backs up the others, even if a pass goes through two of them, the backup player can get it. As soon as the two men are beaten, they should hustle to back up the backup man.

Using the Whole Field

When playing, the whole width of the field should be used. The two wings should be real close to the sidelines. This will cause the other team's defense to spread out to cover them instead of having three or four fullbacks clumped in the middle of the field. When you spread the defense out, you are making it easier for your team to get around them since there are more holes to go through. The ball should be played to the wings when you do this so the other team's fullbacks have to cover them. Your team should pass the ball up the field near the sidelines. When you get down towards the other team's goal, the wing should cross the ball toward the center to a teammate. Then there should be only one or two opponents in the middle of the field with three of your teammates. This would be an easy time to score.

The players can pass the ball as they move forward. If the ball is intercepted, the support man is there to help.

THROUGH PASS

A through pass is really both a pass and a play. A through pass is usually used near the goal mouth when your team is trying to score. It is used by either your halfbacks or your forwards to get the ball through a hole in the opposing defense and into shooting position for a forward.

When you are dribbling the ball, and you see that one of your forwards is ahead of you near an opposing fullback, this is a perfect time to use a through pass. There is probably going to be another fullback ahead and in front of you. Your forward should start to break in between them. As he starts running, pass the ball between the fullbacks, so it goes in front of your player and between him and the goal. Your forward should be able to take a few steps up to the ball and shoot it while the fullbacks are still behind him. This is a very effective play and may result in many scoring opportunities. But, it is hard to get the timing right on this play. Thus, you must practice this over and over again until you get the timing down correctly.

How to Practice It

Practice this play with a friend. Have him run, starting from about the edge of the penalty box, towards the penalty spot in front of the goal. Dribble the ball towards him to about ten yards from the edge of the penalty area. As soon as he starts running, pass the ball in front of him so he can control it and shoot. Keep practicing this move until you get good at it. You might want to use a cone as a defender. Later you can get two people to act as defenders.

MOVING OFF THE BALL

Moving off the ball means running to a spot or moving into position, when you do not have the ball, to create plays or chances to score. You can either move into position to receive a pass, or to decoy opponents in a certain area so that your teammate with the ball can make a more effective pass to someone else. Moving off the ball is very important to your team if it is to become a better attacking unit.

If a teammate has the ball, and you're covered, move quickly to the side, and you may get open for a pass. If the opponent who is guarding you follows you, a teammate might run into your original spot to receive a pass, or the player with the ball can dribble through the hole you have created. Also, by moving quickly, you may open up a hole for the ball to be passed through, to a teammate who is now open and closer to the goal.

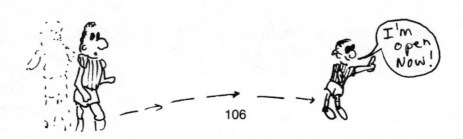

Losing the Ball

As soon as your team loses the ball, everyone must hustle back to defend. If you lose the ball, immediately chase the man with the ball. If you don't regain possession of the ball, this will at least make him rush a pass or lose control of the ball and a teammate can pick it up.

If a passed ball is intercepted by the other team, your teammate nearest to him should immediately chase him to block possible passes that he can make. This is to delay the other team's attack until the rest of your team can get back in position to defend. Your team should always guard an opponent on the goal side of him. Every member of your team should be aware of the space between him and every other member of your team and the distance to the goal. The nearer the attackers come to your goal, the closer they must be marked.

When your opponents have the ball, more of your players should be between the ball and your goal than there are opponents.

Steve sees a teammate and an opponent going for the ball, so he moves away for a pass or a free ball.

Other Ideas on Moving

When your team has the ball, you should have a greater number of teammates near you for possible passes than there are opponents. There should always be a spare man open for you to get a pass to.

You must develop the spirit and stamina to run into position even if the ball doesn't immediately come your way. Be eager to play the ball and help your teammates. This is pretty much what's called "team spirit".

When playing fullback on defense, position yourself so that your opponent has to get around you before he can run for a goal. If you are an outside fullback marking a wing man, try to keep him on the outside, near the touch line. If he tries to dribble around you, make him dribble towards the outside of the field.

When the wing man on the other side of the field has the ball, drop into the middle to cover the space, but keep your eye on the man you are required to cover.

As soon as you are beaten, someone else should cover for you while you quickly run back and cover for him.

The world of soccer is at your feet, but remember it's there for less than a minute each game. What will you do when you don't have the ball?

More Ideas on Practice . . .Switching Play

A good way to practice switching the play is to split your team in half and to scrimmage. Set up four narrow goal areas by using traffic cones, shirts or balls. Put one goal on the penalty line and another even with it on the half-line. The third goal goes half way between the edge of the penalty box and the half-line, in line with the edge of the penalty box, and the fourth goal goes on the other side of the field even with the third goal. Thus, the field is a

Attack goals A, B. Defend goals C, D.
* *If the defenders cover one goal, you can pass back to score at the other.*
* *Don't use a goalie. Keep everyone moving!*
Make sure the field is big enough so you're not crowded.

square with one goal on each side. Your team has to defend two adjacent goals, and score in either of the other two goals, while the other team tries to score in your goals. When you attack one goal, and the opponents' defense blocks you, you have to quickly switch your attack to the other goal. You can pass the ball to a teammate behind you and he quickly turns and tries to score on the other goal. You can also quickly start dribbling toward one goal. As the defending team shifts to stop your attack, change again to the other goal.

Your team can develop different plays by switching the attack from one goal to the other.

This technique gives you good practice for actually switching your attack in an actual game. You can practice noticing when the defense is concentrated on one side of the field. When they are concentrated, you shift your attack to the other side of the field and you will have most of the defenders beaten.

Have your team practice pass plays that you can use in a game. To do this, split your group into three teams with about four or five players on each team. Two teams play at a time. There are no goals. Each team tries to keep the ball away from the other team. Five completed passes in a row by a team without the other team touching the ball is counted as one goal. The object of this exercise is to pass and move the ball around quickly, and to develop pass plays which keep possession of the ball.

Whether you practice in twos or in groups, the idea is to improve, and to have fun doing it!

After you get good at this, your team can play two-touch. In two-touch, each person may only touch the ball twice, then someone else has to touch it. Two-touch teaches you to touch once to control the ball, and once to pass it. In two-touch there can be no dribbling, only passing and moving. When someone touches the ball more than twice, the other team gets possession of the ball. Two-touch is good practice for passing and for rapid pass plays. Your team can even try playing "one-touch" when your skills get better.

Defense Ideas

When your team is on defense, you must cover for each other and restrict the amount of time and space that the other team has to penetrate or to work in.

● As soon as the other team gets the ball, your team must make it hard for the other team to do anything. When the opposing goalie gets the ball, your forwards should mark all the opposing fullbacks tightly. Your halfbacks should mark all the other players in the middle of the field; however, not necessarily as tightly. If the fullback that you are covering receives a ball, quickly hassle him and try to make him rush his play. You must try to block or stop any possible through-pass as your opponents move down the field. When playing halfback, your halfback line can all retreat just enough to make a through-pass difficult. This way if it looks like you

O^1 *has the ball and wants to "break" the defense by a though-pass.* D^1, D^2, *and* D^3, *all retreat toward their own goal.*

might be able to intercept a pass that may go through, you can go for it, or your whole team can quickly run back in front of the other team to produce many barriers threatening the ball. Use whichever one works better for your team all of the time.

● As a fullback, when the opposing attackers get nearer, you should mark them more tightly and limit the space in which they can maneuver towards the goal.

● When a man on your team is beaten, your whole defense should shift to cover for him. He then should run back to cover the space that has been left open, or he should run into position to back up the rest of your defense.

● If you are a halfback or a fullback guarding an opposing player and you are the nearest player on your team to an opposing player who has just beaten one of your teammates, then you must leave the player you are covering and pick up the one with the ball. The nearest teammate to you will then pick up your man, and your beaten teammate will run back to cover for this second teammate.

Ideas for Fullbacks

When you are playing fullback, you have to work together with your other fullbacks to stop the opposing forwards from penetrating. When an opposing player has the ball near you, get in front of him to stop him from breaking towards your goal. Don't get too close to him so that he can trick you and beat you. Try to force him to the outside and away from your goal. If he passes to another player near a teammate, your teammate should now go out to meet him, just as you have just done. Now you drop back to cover the space where the opposing player could possibly make a through-pass, leaving your man a bit open. If the other player passes back to your man, you go forward to meet him again, and your team drops back to cover the space.

If you are the only fullback near two opposing players, you must stay between them. Try to stop the player with the ball from dribbling towards your goal by being in front of him and try to stop him from passing by being slightly towards the side, near the passing lane. If he does pass, then quickly drop back to cover the other player and do the same thing. You must do this until you get help from some of your teammates or until the other team loses the ball or makes a bad pass which your team intercepts. If the other team makes a bad pass, don't go for it unless you're absolutely sure that you can get it. If you miss your try, then they'll beat you. That is bad, especially if the play is near your goal and they can score.

Part Seven

WORDS YOU SHOULD KNOW

Advantage: When a foul occurs but the referee, in his judgment, believes that the team who got fouled will keep possession of the ball without being in danger of the other team immediately taking the ball away, he may use the advantage rule and allow play to continue. He usually does this when stopping play will hurt the team that has been fouled. The rule to remember here is, "play the whistle."

Arc: The quarter-circle at each corner of the field in which the ball is placed for a corner kick.

Attacker: A player trying to score during a game.

Breakaway: When a player has the ball behind the fullbacks and has an open field on which to dribble between him and the goal.

Call: Shouting to a teammate to let him know where you are so he can pass the ball to you. Also, a decision made by a referee.

Centering: Kicking the ball from one of the wings into the goal or penalty area.

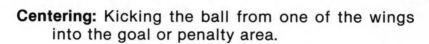

IN PLAY

Charging: (See Shoulder Charge) Attacking an opponent by pushing your shoulder against his shoulder in an attempt to get possession of the ball. The ball must be within playing distance (3 or 4 feet) for you to charge.

Chip: Causing the ball to travel in the air by kicking underneath it.

Chip Pass: A short kick over an opponent's head to a teammate.

Chip Shot: A kick at goal lifted usually over an opposing fullback's or goalkeeper's head.

Coach: The person who gets the team together and organizes and practices with them. He comes to all the games and shouts "GO TEAM" to the players. He tells them how to play. He tells the players what position to play.

Corner Kick: A kick taken at the corner of the field by the attacking team when the defending team last touched the ball before it crossed the goal line.

Cover: Guarding a player on the other team to stop him from getting the ball.

Crossbar: The goal bar which is parallel to the ground.

Dangerous Play: Any play, movement or action that puts an opponent, a teammate or yourself in a position where you may get injured.

Dribbling: Moving the ball with the foot with successive kicks.

Defense: The part of your team trying to stop the other team from scoring.

Far Post: The goalpost that is farthest away from the kicker.

Forwards: The people on your team who take most of the shots and do most of the scoring.

Foul: An illegal play or movement by a player.

Free-kick: A free-kick is given to a team when the other team commits a foul. The ball is placed on the ground to be kicked from the spot where the foul occurred. A free-kick gives you a chance to pass or shoot the ball while all the players on the other team must remain at least ten yards away from the ball until it goes its circumference.

Goal: When the ball goes between the goalposts to score a point, that's called a goal.

Goal Box: The box in which the ball is placed to take a goal kick. Also called goal area.

Goalie: The one player on your team who is allowed to touch the ball with his hands in the penalty area. His job is to stop the ball from going into the goal and to get the ball to another player on your team.

Goalkick: A free kick taken by the defending team when the attacking team kicks the ball across the goal line (unless a goal is scored).

Goal Line: The line between the two corner flags on each end of the field.

Goalmouth: The area immediately in front of the goal.

Goalposts: The posts that make up the goal. Also called uprights.

Halfback: The players on your team who play around the middle of the field. They pass the ball to the forwards so they can score.

TIP: Goalie is Responsible for organizing the defense.

Half-line: The line across the middle of the field which divides the field in half.

Half-time: A game is divided into two equally timed halves. After the half is up, a short break is taken and the teams switch sides of the field and the goal they are defending.

Half Volley: A ball kicked as soon as the ball starts rising from a bounce.

Heading: Propelling the ball by hitting it with the head.

Instep Drive: A kick or shot taken with the part of the foot where your shoelaces are located.

Linesman: The person near one of the touchlines who waves his flag to signal the ball being out-of-bounds or a player being offside.

Marking: Covering or guarding a particular opponent.

Near Post: The goalpost nearest to the kicker.

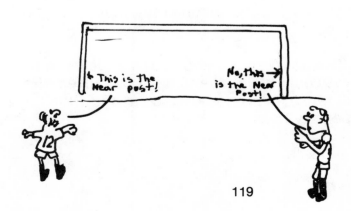

If it weren't for the Net, I'd have chased 20 balls today!

When you Pass, Accuracy is Important!

Net: The plastic or string-like thing that is tied to the goalposts to make it easier to tell when a goal is scored.

Offense: The part of your team trying to score.

Opponent: The person or people on the other team in a game.

Off-the-Ball: Running without the ball to move into an open space so you can receive a pass or to help a teammate receive a pass.

Offside: This means being ahead of the ball when it is played in your direction. In order for you to be judged "offside", you must be in the attacking half and have fewer than two opponents ahead of you. The referee decides whether to call it when the ball is played by a teammate.

Parents: The people who take you to all the games and cheer you on.

Pass: Using part of your body to hit the ball to a teammate.

Penalty Box: The lines which form the rectangle in which the goalie may use his hands to touch the ball. It's the second rectangle in front of the goal.

Penalty Kick: A shot on goal inside the penalty area with only the goalie to beat. It is given after the defense has committed a foul inside the penalty box.

Power Kick: A hard, fast shot or kick.

Referee: The person who controls the soccer game and blows his whistle when there is a foul.

Restarts: The process of starting play again after it has been stopped; for example after a goal, or after the ball went out-of-bounds.

Score: A ball going under the crossbar and between the goalposts, completely crossing the goal line.

Screening: When dribbling, keeping your body between the ball and the person trying to take it away so he won't be able to take it away.

Shot: An attempt to score a goal.

Shoulder Charge: (See Charging) Using your shoulder by leaning against the shoulder of an opponent, to push him off balance so you can gain possession of the ball.

Side Volley: A ball played while still in the air.

Slide Tackle: Gaining possession of the ball by kicking it away from the opponent's feet while you are sliding on the ground.

Strikers: The forwards in the middle of the forward line who are trying to score and who usually take the most shots.

Substitute: A player on a team who is not playing at the beginning of a game but will probably go in some time.

THROW-IN

FRONT VIEW

Sweeper: If yo   ullbacks, they may play   weeper is the defender   cial player to mark an   he other fullbacks to back them up.

Tackling: Using the feet to take the ball away from an opposing player.

Tactics: Strategy used and plays made in an attempt to out-play the other team.

BACK VIEW

Throw-in: When the ball goes out-of-bounds, across the touchline, it must be put back into play. To do this a throw-in is used. A throw-in is made by holding the ball with both hands behind the head. Then the hands are brought forward to throw the ball.

Touchlines

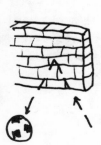

Touchline: The lines on the long side of the field which indicate the boundaries.

Trapping: The act of gaining control of a moving ball by stopping it with a part of the body.

Tripping: Causing an opponent to fall by hitting his feet out from beneath him.

Volley: Kicking the ball while it is still in the air.

Wall-pass: This is a play for going around an opponent. You pass the ball to a teammate while you continue to run forward past an opponent. As soon as your teammate gets the ball, he passes it back to you.

Wing: Either the forward parts of the field towards the sidelines or the forward who plays on that part of the field.

122